DIAGNOSTIC INTERVIEWING FOR CONSULTANTS AND AUDITORS

A Participative Approach
to Problem Solving

John Quay

QUAY ASSOCIATES   Columbus, Ohio

Library of Congress Cataloging-in-Publication Data

Quay, John.
  Diagnostic interviewing for consultants and auditors.

  1. Interviewing. 2. Personnel management.
3. Management. 4. Business consultants.
5. Interviewing in auditing. I. Title.
HF5549.5.I6Q38   1986   658.3'1124   86-443
ISBN 0-9616062-0-7

QUAY, JOHN
Diagnostic Interviewing for Consultants and Auditors
Quay Associates

A Participative Approach to Problem Solving

Printed in the United States of America

10   9   8   7   6   5

Quay Associates
Box 18052
Columbus, Ohio 43218

FOREWORD

This book is the result of a combination of circumstances: my extensive training and experience as an employment interviewer, and my participation in the design of a program to diagnose general management problems. Early in my career I was trained to evaluate candidates for employment by Dick Fear of the Psychological Corporation.* The techniques I learned from Mr. Fear included planning the interview, setting the stage, breaking the ice, generating a flow of spontaneous information, the use of questions to guide the interview and probe into pay dirt areas, and how to soften questions on sensitive subjects.

Later in my career, as a consultant with a major CPA firm I helped to design a general management survey program to familiarize both auditors and consultants with the operations, key personnel, assets, and problems of major clients. It was hoped that such familiarization would solidify working relationships, broaden the perspective of the auditors and consultants involved, and lead to an occasional consulting assignment. The program achieved all of its objectives.

In the process of preparing the survey teams, I discovered some apprehension on the part of the younger auditors and consultants about interviewing top managers at client companies. The cause of this apprehension turned out to be lack of confidence regarding how to question a senior executive in a function the auditor or consultant knew nothing about.

To resolve this problem, I instituted an interview training program which taught trainees how to use very general questions ("Tell me about . . ." your major responsibilities, your organization, issues facing

---

* Mr. Richard Fear is author of *The Evaluation Interview*, published by McGraw-Hill Book Company, New York, 1958.

iii

your industry, etc.) followed up by "encouragers" borrowed from Dick Fear's evaluation interview ("Uh-huh," "That's very interesting," etc.). We also taught the group how to use probing questions to dig into pay dirt areas ("Tell me a little more about . . . ," "I'd be interested in learning more about . . ." etc.), and summary statements to move the interview along ("That gives me a good picture of your major responsibilities. Next I'd like to cover your organization. Tell me about . . .").

These techniques, together with some role playing—we were able to get some client Presidents and Vice Presidents to act as guinea pigs— turned our reluctant novices into more confident interviewers, and our program was off and running. In fact, this training worked so well that it was included in all subsequent general management survey planning stages and given at special training programs for consultants, auditors, and even the audit departments of our client companies.

As an independent consultant, I have continued to develop this program, adapting it to various audiences. It has been conducted for state chapters of the Institute of Internal Auditors, the Association of Internal Management Consultants, various client operations audit and troubleshooting groups, and it is a regular feature of the Fundamentals of Management Consulting Seminar offered by the Institute of Management Consultants.

In the course of presenting this program to different audiences, I have learned from many people. Beyond my major obligation to Dick Fear, both novice and seasoned consultants have offered case examples, experiences and better answers or solutions to interview situations. Formulating hypotheses, using first names, interpreting body language, handling confidential disclosures, and the pros and cons of feedback discussions with department heads are just some of the subjects to which class participants have contributed ideas and insights. Like most teachers, I have learned more than I taught.

The idea of putting this program into book form resulted from my research of the literature. Libraries, journals and magazine indices turned up many books and articles on consulting—how to solve problems, write reports, market your talents, manage a firm, make presentations, etc., and much writing on the subject of interviewing—for social workers, ministers, lawyers, journalists, decision makers, and even police interrogators. No extensive publishing has been done, however, on interviewing for consultants or management/operations auditors. Ergo, this book.

This is a skill book. It does not deal with the content or substance of consulting: how to design an information system, lay out a plant, select a computer, conduct a marketing study or develop a business plan. As a skill book, its focus is on techniques which are best demonstrated by illustrations. These should be taken for what they are—illustrations, and not models or standards. There is no one best way to do things in interpersonal relations. What works for me may not work for you; and what works for both of us in one situation may not work for either of us in a similar situation. Each of us has his own style, and every situation is different.

This book, then, should be viewed as a starting point, not a definitive work. The examples are suggestive. With experience everyone—especially intuitive people—will get the hang of it and try out their own ways of handling interview situations. To paraphrase an old adage, if it works for you, it's perfect.

CONTENTS

Chapter 1

INTRODUCTION

All of us are diagnosticians. We look to the sky for signs of coming weather. We troubleshoot our aches and pains for symptoms of a cold, the flu, or something more serious. Some of us can even diagnose problems with our cars by just listening to their engines.

In business, too, anyone with a few years' experience can detect signs of trouble, begin to pinpoint causes and come up with ideas for improvement. At first these ideas may not be appropriate to the problem. The solutions may be too simple for a very complex situation, and the prescriptions may treat symptoms rather than causes. With time and more experience, however, we will improve our batting average. Indeed, most of the world's businesses survive because the people in them have learned to properly diagnose their problems and correct them.

This book is written to assist special kinds of business diagnosticians—problem solvers from outside the company or department who must, usually on short notice and within a limited time frame, gather sufficient data, analyze them and come up with solutions or conclusions. These "outsiders" may be:

- consultants, including internal company consultants, troubleshooters, or project/task force problem solvers, or

- auditors, especially of the operations or management variety, from inside or outside the company.

Because the consultants and auditors (called hereafter "consultants") are new to their situations, and because their time frame for gathering data is limited, they all must collect as much relevant information as they can as quickly as they can. To do this they must use one or more of the following data gathering methods:

DATA GATHERING METHODS

Observation

Observation or inspection, usually includes a plant or office tour to get impressions of such things as work pace, layout, and so on. This direct observation has many advantages. It can take as much or as little time as the consultant needs for a fix on the problem or situation. It is first hand information versus hearsay or reports by others. And, for the expert, it may be all the consultant needs to find what is wrong, or where significant improvements can be made. Because of these advantages, observation is usually a part of most engagements.

The limitations of observation or inspection are (1) it does not get at the thinking behind an activity or program—the human problems, reasoning processes or plans of the personnel involved, and (2) observation itself, as in the classic Hawthorne studies, sometimes alters the behavior of those observed.

Materials Collection

Materials collection includes organization charts, policy manuals, annual reports, job descriptions, information system outputs, and so on. (Consultants are by instinct kleptomaniacs). Virtually every engagement involves material collection of some kind. To the extent that figures, charts, and reports are accurate, they provide the kind of "hard" evidence consultants need to document their findings. Their limitations are (1) they seldom deal comprehensively with solutions to problems, and (2) written materials, almost by definition, lack the spontaneity and free flowing discussion so necessary to paint in the odd corners and details of a problem, and to brainstorm ideas for improvement.

Surveys

Surveys or questionnaires cover attitudes, information needs, reports received, customers called on, time spent on various tasks, and so on. Surveys have the singular merit of collecting facts or opinions from many sources simultaneously. If the consultant can reduce his* information requirements to specific questions, he can save everyone's time and money. This approach is ideal for determining attitudes, employee or customer preferences, audience reactions, and even individuals 'feelings or beliefs.

Surveys, however, suffer from statistical error problems and may be difficult to analyze or interpret when used to probe complex issues, or require essay type responses. They also do not provide for interaction between the consultant and respondents who raise interesting observations or give provocative answers which the consultant may wish to probe.

Interviews

Interviews are almost always combined with other data gathering methods because they overcome the limitations previously listed. Interviews are flexible. Properly used, they can cover facts as well as opinions. The interview can be used to probe sensitive areas, take into account non-

---

* The male pronoun is used throughout this book for the sake of readability.

verbal cues, and follow up on promising leads as they emerge in the discussion. For diagnosticians, the interview is the most effective method of data gathering because it enables the interviewer to engage the thinking, judgments and problem solving abilities of the interviewee. As stated at the outset of this chapter, most employees are diagnosticians, and, if two heads are better than one, why not twenty, or fifty— especially when many of the interviewees have an intimate knowledge of the company and its problems. Often they may also develop solutions or at least promising ideas for improvements. If prophets are without honor in their own countries, employees also go unheard in their own companies. The consultant, whose interviews can tap this rich reservoir of viewpoints and information, gains both a broad perspective on the problems, and a wide spectrum of answers from which to formulate his best recommendations.

Good interviewing, like a good game of golf, requires frequent practice and periodic fine tuning. Even professional golfers find it useful to occasionally go back to the basics—stance, head position, grip, and swing. This book addresses the fundamentals of diagnostic interviewing. While intended for beginners, it may also be useful to seasoned consultants who would like to compare their successful techniques with those presented here, or who would like a refresher, or who may never have had interview training and would like to check up on their self-taught methods. Still others may have gotten into poor habits such as:

- impatience or wanting to get too quickly into crucial issues
- developing a kind of quiz or fixed line of questioning to identify weak managers, inadequate planning, or some other factor which in their experience is often at the root of client problems
- using their interviews to opine, argue, and even challenge interviewees regarding their management views, style, or philosophy, or

- getting sloppy about note taking during their interviews and trying to reconstruct key points after a long
  day of interviewing.

These problems indicate the need to return to basics.
It is hoped, therefore, that both beginners and experienced
consultants will find these fundamentals helpful.

The format of the book addresses the steps and processes involved in preparing for and conducting diagnostic
interviews. In addition to the illustrations in the text, ex-
tended examples from actual interviews are included to
give the reader a better sense of how various techniques
are used in a fuller context. The appendices are devoted
to exercises and drills which can be practiced in a group
under supervision, or, in many cases, performed alone.
Some "better" answers to these exercises are included at
the end.

Chapter 2

DESIGNING THE INTERVIEW PLAN

Like speeches or reports, the interview needs an outline or plan designed to accomplish its purposes. For the inexperienced interviewer a comprehensive interview plan should include:

- a statement of the purposes or objectives
- selection of the appropriate interview type or approach
- formulation and sequencing of the topical areas to be covered and/or the specific facts to be elicited, and
- preparation of a lead statement, and lead questions and follow up questions for each topical area to be covered.

OBJECTIVES

All interviews have one or more purposes. The purpose may be to determine the scope and severity of problems in order to write a proposal. It could be to explore the information needs of the company so that a proper management information system can be designed and implemented. Or, the interview purpose may be to assess the adequacy of control procedures to assure compliance with company policies. In many cases ancillary objectives are also involved, such as: evaluating key personnel, promoting good client relations, laying the groundwork for change, or uncovering opportunities for operations improvements which are related or unrelated to the major purpose of the engagement. The interview plan should state these purposes at the outset. For example:

"To assess the effectiveness of the Engineering Department and recommend centralization, decentralization (to projects), or some combination as most appropriate. Also, to identify one or more leaders or potential leaders in the organization."

INTERVIEW APPROACHES

Once the purpose of the interview has been determined, a proper format or interview approach should be selected from among those following.

Directive

If the interview is exclusively or primarily aimed at eliciting facts, then a directive or question/answer approach is most appropriate. In this interview approach, the consultant questions the interviewee regarding numbers, events, dates, records, and so on. (Dick Fear calls this the "Perry Mason" approach since it resembles the interrogation of a witness on the stand.) The directive interview has the merit of covering a maximum amount of information in a minimum time. It is ideally suited to compliance auditing where a specific series of questions or checks can be completed to determine whether a system, procedure, or operation is being performed as intended.*

The primary drawback of the directive interview is that it does not elicit opinions, judgments or evaluations from the interviewee. Often, the respondent becomes so conditioned to waiting for the next question that he is *discouraged* from offering gratuitous opinions or amplifying statements.

Non-Directive

At the other extreme, the non-directive interview approach seeks to open up a large area for exploration and discussion—for example, business strategies—and encourages the interviewee to ramble along on this subject in any way he chooses. The advantage of this approach is that it brings out a great deal of spontaneous information, including opinions, judgments and evaluative comments. The non-directive approach is most useful when time is available, and the occasion presents itself, for example in connection with drinks, dinner, and an evening of discussion, or a long trip with a key client executive.

The disadvantage of the non-directive interview is that it is very time consuming. Lacking direction and control, it tends to wander over many unfruitful topics before arriving at the critical material which is germane to the engagement.

The Pattern Interview

Consultants will find the pattern or structured type of interview approach most appropriate for diagnostic purposes. This approach is directive in that it focuses the interview on preselected areas or topics for discussion. It is

---

* For lists of appropriate questions for this type of interview see *Management Auditing/A Questionnaire Approach*, by Robert Thierauf, AMACOM, 1983. Also see, *Modern Accounting and Auditing Checklists*, edited by Loscalzo & Wendell, published by Warren Gorham & Lamont, Boston, Mass.

non-directive in allowing the interviewee to explore each topic in any way he sees fit. The pattern interview encourages the interviewee to express viewpoints and evaluations. Facts, supporting evidence, and supplementary data are solicited along the way as necessary or at the conclusion of each topical discussion.

The advantages of the pattern interview are that it not only conserves time and effort by focusing on the key engagement issues, but also provides ample opportunity and encouragement for interviewees to express their ideas and opinions. These advantages make this interview approach ideal for both diagnosing problems and generating ideas for solutions—the "raison d'être" of most consulting engagements and operations audits. Accordingly, the primary emphasis in this book is placed on the pattern or structured type of interview.

INTERVIEW TOPICS

Once the consultant has determined his objectives and selected his interview approach, he needs to formulate the topics or subject areas to be covered in each interview. Interview topics for the pattern interview are determined by (1) the engagement objectives or problems to be solved, (2) homework, and (3) the formulation of hypotheses based on 1 and 2.

Engagement Objectives

Engagement objectives are usually provided by the client, such as, "My organization is top heavy. I need help in pruning it." "We want to know what the market thinks of our product—and what we will have to do to improve it." Sometimes objectives are derivable from known data and/or directed by top management, for example, "Division X's profits have been dropping for the past six months. Get in there and find out what's wrong." Or, internal consultants and operations auditors may have regularly scheduled divisions or departments to visit on a general exploratory basis. This is like the general physical checkup one gets periodically from the doctor.

Homework

How ever the engagement objectives are determined, the consultant should do what homework he can before going on site to conduct interviews (other than scoping interviews which normally precede a proposal or engagement). This homework may have several purposes:

- The consultant may need to become familiar with the client company, industry, technology and market-place—unless he is already an expert in this field or an internal consultant/auditor. To do this, he can read company literature, competitors' ads, articles, and editorials in industry or association journals. Editors of such journals take pains to stay abreast of the issues and hot news items of interest to their readers. There may be regular columns on government regulations, foreign competition, opportunities, new technology, etc. The ads can tell the reader what new products or services are coming on stream, and sometimes what kinds of job talents are in demand.

- Homework is also needed to assess the client's particular assets and problem areas. These are identifiable from annual reports, 10-Ks, industry data, audit papers, and other information furnished by the client. For example, the consultant can determine that the company has a higher than industry growth rate, but lower profitability than its competitors; that the scrap rate has been rising while the rate of capital reinvestment has been declining; or that three new products were launched five years ago, but none since.

- Finally, homework should include a review of organization charts, names, titles, ages, selected policies, report samples, business plans, and other available information which would be pertinent to the consultant's areas of investigation.

Hypotheses

Based on the objectives of the engagement and his home-work on the client, the consultant is in a position to develop hypotheses regarding likely causes of the problems identified. To illustrate, a client was concerned about losing market share and the consultant's research showed this to be a significant trend. The consultant hypothesized several likely causes: poor product, poor service, high price, poor distribution, lack of sales incentives, lack of training or high turnover among salesmen, and poor sales or marketing management. Based on these hypothesized causes, the consultant designed his interview to cover the following topics: product, sales organization, marketing strategy, and sales and service effectiveness.

The chief cause of the problem turned out to be none of the ones hypothesized—it was poor company image. Nevertheless, these hypotheses enabled the consultant to focus his interviews around the likeliest topics to prove or disprove one or more of his assumptions. Further probing during these interviews identified the primary cause of market slippage and enabled him to prescribe an appropriate solution.

Sometimes specific questions will confirm or disprove an hypothesis: "Is your pay here competitive with local and industry practice?" Usually, however, hypotheses will need discussion and probing to determine not just their validity, but also the extent of their validity: "You say your turnover rate here is 12%. How does that compare with your competition, your past experience, and your own sense of what an appropriate rate should be?"

TYPICAL TOPICS

For most engagements the topics selected will be the same for all interviews with some special additions and deletions due to functional specialties or level in the organization, such as, policy formulation at the top, and clerical productivity at lower levels. In every interview it is im-

portant to know where the interviewee is coming from—
his position, responsibilities and place in the organization.
These factors locate his perspective or viewpoint regarding
the company's problems and possible solutions. Therefore,
most interview plans should include the topics of the interviewee's position, major responsibilities, and his organization—whom he reports to and who reports to him.

Depending on the problems identified and the con-
comitant hypotheses, additional topics might be:

- the interviewee's relationships and communications
  issues with superiors, subordinates, peers, and outsiders
- the interviewee's education, experience, assets, shortcomings, career objectives and development needs
- the goals or performance standards in the company,
  department, and the interviewee's position
- company products—their advantages and vulnerabil-
  ities
- customers, competitors, market share, and trends
- planning and budgeting
- information systems—current and needed
- financial controls
- policies and procedures
- company or department climate, morale, motivation,
  and reward systems.

For all but the bleakest client situations, a good topic
to cover is assets—things the company or department has
going for it. These might include such things as talent,
reputation, facilities, cash reserves, technology, market
dominance, and so on. Discussing assets gives the consultant some ideas of the strengths he can build on. Such
a discussion also gives the interviewee a feeling that he is
presenting a more balanced picture of his company or department.

A good topic on which to end the interview is the
interviewee's ideas about solutions for the problems he has
discussed. By covering this topic in all his interviews the

consultant can access and evaluate the best thinking from several levels and viewpoints in the client organization.

Other topics could be added to this list. Or, in the case of a tightly focused engagement, any of the topics listed above might be divided into several subtopics. For most engagements, however, five or six subject areas is a reasonable limit for a one or two hour pattern interview. High level executives will take longer, while lower level employees can be covered in less time. Large complex problem areas take longer, while smaller pinpointed problems need less time. Whatever the size or complexity of the assignment, careful topic selection is essential to focus the interviewee's attention, while staying within reasonable time limitations.

TOPICAL SEQUENCE

Once the topics have been selected, they should be sequenced according to the following guidelines:

- from familiar/known to less familiar/debatable
- from simple to complex
- from impersonal/neutral to personal/sensitive.

The reason for these guidelines is that in any new encounter both parties need time to get to know each other and begin to establish trust. If asked to launch immediately into an analysis of problems—especially complex ones—or an assessment of one's superior's shortcomings, many interviewee's will become guarded and may even remain silent. If, on the other hand, a familiar and neutral topic such as the interviewee's position is used to start the interview, both parties can use the five or ten minutes this subject requires to feel each other out. The consultant will quickly discern whether the interviewee is shy, garrulous, defensive, or confident. He can often determine as well if the interviewee is a perceptive and analytical person who can be of real help in defining and solving problems, or a shallow thinker who won't have much to offer.

Based on these early clues, the consultant can adjust his approach for the rest of the interview. He can be especially encouraging and supportive of shy types. He can move more quickly to sensitive topics with open and confident types, and he can shorten the interview for "dry wells" (those who don't really know much about what is going on).

From the interviewee's point of view, a subject such as his major responsibilities is easy to talk about while he sizes up the consultant. Is he really interested in what I do? Does he understand the importance of my role around here? Can I trust him?

Starting with the interviewee's job and major responsibilities has the further advantage of reassurance in those cases where the consultant may be viewed with suspicion or anxiety. If the engagement is the interviewee's first exposure to consultants he may not know what to expect. Will I be grilled? Will he ask me things I don't know? What will he do with the information I give him? Am I being evaluated for possible layoff?

When the consultant begins by asking about the interviewee's job, shows real interest in his responsibilities, goes out of the way to compliment accomplishments, and is sympathetic about the frustrations or difficulties of getting the job done—the interviewee should conclude: (1) I expected that the consultant might ask about what I do, and he did—I feel more comfortable and reassured; (2) this experience isn't going to be so bad after all; and, (3) now that the consultant understands my role here, he can properly value my views and ideas about this place.

An appropriate following topic might be organization, unless this was covered by the interviewee as part of his discussion of position. In either case, once a good relationship has been established, the interview can address its primary goal—the exploration of the problem areas which gave rise to the engagement.

The interviewee's ideas regarding solutions or improvements is a good final topic for each interview. By this time the interviewee should be feeling comfortable, secure and expansive. He should be glad to contribute ideas and help out in any way possible.

FOLLOW UP QUESTIONS

In the usual case, several of the topics selected will focus on specific problem areas to test the consultant's hypotheses. The novice interviewer will need a way to remind himself that he wants to cover some specific views or facts in these topical areas. This is easily done by listing follow up questions or points to cover under each topical heading. For example, if the topic is quality control follow up questions might include: where does the function report, how are standards set, the qualifications and training of inspectors, the use of statistical quality control techniques, and data on returns, rejects and warranty costs.

Most of these and other pertinent points will be covered by the interviewee in his discussion of this topic. By referring to his follow up questions the consultant can pick up on any key points which may have been omitted.

The interview plan now has a statement of purpose; the interview approach to be used; a list of topics or subject areas to be covered, including the appropriate sequence from the familiar or neutral to the debatable or sensitive; and a list of follow up questions for those topics which bear most directly on the likely problems. To complete the interview plan, the apprentice consultant should write out a lead statement and lead questions for each topic or subject area to be covered.

LEAD STATEMENT

The lead statement tells the interviewee the purpose of the engagement, the major topics to be covered, and the approximate time which will be required for the interview. Prior to the interview each interviewee should have been told or received a notice explaining the purpose of the engagement, the name of the consultant or auditor who will be conducting the interviews, and the general areas or topics to be covered.* It is important that the lead statement match this advance notice quite closely. Interviewees can become upset by discrepencies between what their superiors have told them and what the consultant says. Conversely, it is reassuring to have the interview start out as expected.

Following is a typical lead statement:

> "As Mr. Alford's letter indicated, Mrs. Brown, your division was selected for a management audit this year, focusing on the security of our computer systems. For the next hour or so I'd like to cover with you your computer department organization, the major programs now running, the security measures you've taken, and any plans you have for the future of this function."

LEAD QUESTIONS

Lead questions should be prepared as part of the interview plan to be sure they are clear and sufficiently general to give the interviewee a wide enough range in which to roam around spontaneously. For example, if the topic is assets, it would be a poor start to ask, "What is the most important asset this company has?" This question requires that the interviewee know what is meant by "assets"— is it balance sheet items, products, people, or what, exactly? Also, it asks that he mentally evaluate these assets and select the most important one. Finally, this type of question can be answered by a word or phrase. It is not asked in such a way that the interviewee is encouraged to become discursive on this subject.

---

* On rare occasions, e.g., an adversary audit situation, the consultant may wish to conduct a surprise visit and hope to uncover information the client hasn't had time to hide by a carefully constructed cover. For tips on handling these interviews see, *The Gentle Art of Interviewing and Interrogation,* by Royal & Schutt, Prentice Hall, Inc. Englewood Cliffs, N.J., 1976.

Instead, to cover this topic a better approach would be, "Let's talk next about what's good about this company, the real plusses or advantages that enable you to compete successfully. What would you say some of these things are?" If your meaning is still not clear, a suggestive laundry list type question can be helpful: "Is it people, marketing organization, quality, or what?" This wording encourages the interviewee to start in anywhere and cover the subject as he sees fit.

In the unusual case where some ranking of assets is desired (e.g., to sample employee understanding of the importance of quality), this can be left to the end of the discussion on this topic. Then the consultant can ask, "Of those assets you have mentioned, which do you think is most important?" Or, "How would you rank the importance of the four assets you have mentioned?"

Properly worded lead questions for each topic are important to eliciting broad ranging responses. For this reason novice interviewers are urged to think through and write out these lead questions in advance. This drill should also serve to remind them of the planned sequence of topics to be covered during the pattern interview.

ACRONYM REMINDER

A helpful way to remember the proper sequence of topics in an interview is to use an acronym such as the following:

R esponsibilities

O rganization

G oals or plans for the future

A ssets

P roblems

I deas for solutions

Here the acronym, ROGAPI, written in the margin of one's notes, serves as a reminder of both the topics to be covered and the planned order or sequence.

CONCLUSION

Inexperienced interviewers should write out their interview plan including purpose, type of interview, topics to be covered, follow up questions, lead statement, and lead questions. This plan should be reviewed with a superior or coach for the first few engagements, or until appropriate phrasings become comfortable and automatic.

Appendix A provides a sample interview plan and several suggested cases for practice in designing interview plans.

Chapter 3

ENCOURAGING TRUST AND SPONTANEOUS RESPONSE

To do their job most effectively consultants must not only get the facts, they must also get the best thinking, judgments, and ideas of key client personnel. What are the underlying problems, who and/or what factors are the causes of these problems, and what will it take to remedy the situation? These issues are the essence of every engagement. The more open and straightforward the responses one can obtain from informed insiders, the more accurately and promptly will the consultant be able to diagnose and prescribe effective solutions.

Getting open and spontaneous responses from interviewees doesn't mean the consultant is after unanalyzed or sloppy thinking. It means he is looking for information that is free of defensiveness, does not avoid sensitive areas, and is not colored by the interviewee's fear of reprisals. To

19

accomplish this, the consultant must quickly establish an atmosphere of trust, and encourage a spontaneous flow of discourse on the part of the interviewee.

CREATING TRUST

Trust between consultant and interviewee is a function of (1) their understanding of the need for cooperation; (2) the chemistry or makeup of the parties involved; and (3) the past experiences of the interviewee with consultants.

Understanding

Regarding understanding, the consultant should set the stage properly by his opening remarks so that the interviewee is made aware of the purpose and importance of the interview for the improvement and welfare of the operation, department or company. In potentially sensitive situations, it may also be necessary to reassure the interviewee that his remarks will be kept in confidence or lumped with others in such a way that he will not be personally identified.

Chemistry

As to chemistry, or makeup of the two parties involved in an interview, the consultant can only control his approach and hope that the interviewee will respond appropriately. In general, people respond well to warmth, friendliness, encouragement, receptivity, acceptance, and understanding. Conversely, they are turned off by aloofness, disagreement, disapproval, disdain, boredom, and a loud or overbearing manner. It is the consultant's task to create, as quickly as possible, an atmosphere of cooperation and collaboration so that both he and the interviewee can focus on a joint problem solving effort.

Past Experience

Past experience is the most difficult aspect of trust to deal with. Interviewees who have learned to trust people in general and consultants in particular are apt to be open and forthright. Obviously the converse is also true. Since the consultant is normally unaware of the interviewee's past experience, he should approach each interview as though he were making a friend. In so doing he should be aware that the consultant-interviewee relationship must pass through several stages as follows:

- who are you and what do you want?
- I'll tell you about facts and events
- I'll provide general opinions and judgments
- I'll offer specific opinions and judgments
- I'll share my personal feelings and views about what's going on around here — people, problems, etc.

Confident interviewees will proceed quickly through these stages. However, others need more time before they will admit a stranger into their private world. The consultant must be careful not to rush this process if he is to gain the trust of these individuals.

Other Factors

While the consultant should do his best to win the trust and cooperation of each interviewee, there are several factors which provide additional motivation for some employees to assist in the problem solving process:

- most people enjoy a captive audience—especially one who is vitally interested in learning all he can about the company, its products, people and problems
- many people have ideas about what is wrong with the world, but it's all too seldom that they get a chance to prescribe solutions—especially to someone in a position to do something with their ideas, and

- for a few, there is the hope that their perceptions and proposals will win them the recognition and possibly advancement they deserve. In fact, almost every engagement does turn up a few heroes—prophets who have correctly pinpointed the issues and tried to get them addressed, despite their company's unwillingness to listen or take them seriously.

ENCOURAGING SPONTANEOUS FLOW

The process of encouraging a spontaneous flow of discourse begins even before the interview starts. As stated earlier, most engagements are preceded by a notice or announcement which prepares those employees who will be interviewed for the consultant's arrival. This notice should state the purpose and importance of the engagement; the name of the firm and/or the consultant(s) who will be doing the interviewing; request the employee's cooperation and candor; if reprisals are a possible issue, assure the confidentiality of their remarks; indicate the major topics to be covered; and note the approximate time required for each interview. The consultants involved should participate in wording this announcement, and see that their lead statement closely matches this notice.

Creating the Right Atmosphere

The consultant starts creating an atmosphere the second he walks through the door. It goes without saying that there should be a door to a room that can be closed off. Privacy, for diagnostic interviewing, is essential, including a cutoff or interception of phone calls, if possible.

In addition to privacy, the best atmosphere for most diagnostic interviews requires that the consultant be receptive. He should become the audience while the interviewee assumes the pulpit. Since interviews are normally conducted sitting down, it is important that the consultant's posture in a chair also be receptive. This impression will be facilitated by sitting back rather than leaning forward (a more assertive, even aggressive position), while taking notes unobtrusively on his lap rather than on the desk or table.

The consultant also contributes to creating the right atmosphere by doing and saying the expected thing. He dresses the way business professionals in this part of the country are expected to dress. His opening remarks are conventional, again what most people would expect. A loud voice, unusual dress or strange behavior is upsetting to many interviewees, and, once upset, many valuable minutes may be required to create the reassuring, unsuspicious atmosphere so critical to spontaneous discourse.

Breaking the Ice

Appointments should be made by each consultant or by the department head of each employee to be interviewed. Department heads may actually introduce the consultant to each employee or the consultant may introduce himself. In either case, the first minute or two in the interviewee's presence are important in setting the stage and should be devoted to breaking the ice. Ice breaking is expected in any friendly new encounter. Its use in the interview situation starts things off in a familiar and reassuring fashion. Most importantly, however, it gets the interviewee talking spontaneously, a prelude to the discursive type of interchange which will follow.

Most people have learned how to break the ice with strangers as a part of their social experience. If so, their instincts are generally a good guide. However, there are some DOs and DON'Ts which apply to the interview situation.

DO: use the most common and expected topics—the weather, any unusual features about the office or difficulties in finding it, conversation pieces on the interviewee's desk, an obvious hobby—such as a mounted fish, amateur paintings, or a series of photographs—or an unusual view from the window.

DON'T: get into long stories or jokes (but a little facetious humor is helpful), play "who do you know" regarding his company or your firm (a close friend may know too much, an enemy will put him on guard), get into politics, religion or potentially controversial topics, or let the ice breaking go on for more than two or three minutes.

At a convenient break the consultant should launch into his lead statement followed immediately by the lead question for the first topic of the pattern interview.

Encouragers

A spontaneous flow of information is stimulated by a focused combination of facial and verbal encouragers. People who are skilled in interpersonal relations have learned, often at an early age, how to stimulate interest and enthusiasm on the part of others. Intuitively and perhaps without awareness of how they do it, they

- appear receptive, with eyebrows up (eyebrows down mean, "I don't believe you"), a slight smile, and an open and expectant expression

- focus full attention on the other person, including maintaining good eye contact

- nod periodically and make verbal acknowledgments of what they hear—"uh-huh," "yes," "is that so," "of course,"etc.

- respond by verbal acknowledgment even when they don't agree e.g. "I see," "I understand what you are saying," etc. (understanding is not the same as concurrence)

- give appropriate "pats" or praise to the other person's accomplishments and good ideas—"good for you," "I certainly agree," "that's very perceptive of you," "that was an impressive achievement," "you certainly were persistent," etc.

- play down the bad or unfortunate news—"what a bad break," "it could have happened to anyone," "I'm sure you had your reasons," "that must have been hard on all of you," etc.
- reflect the speaker's feeling or mood, whether happy or sad, and
- inject occasional humor when appropriate via a facetious comment or gentle gibe; jokes and serious barbs are taboo.

When these powerful encouragers are combined and focused on the interviewee, especially early in the interview, the result is often such a spontaneous flow of discourse that it is sometimes difficult to shut off or control!

CONCLUSION

There will always be holdouts, people who won't or can't open up or cooperate. Fortunately, these are few. Chapter 7 deals with these and other special situations. For most interviewees, however, the creation of trust and the focused application of conversation encouragers is sufficient to evoke the interviewee's natural desire to be of help, and to do so with openness, spontaneity, and candor. Consultants cannot hope for more than this from their interviews.

Exhibit 1 illustrates some of the techniques which have been presented to encourage trust and spontaneous response.

Exhibit 1

GETTING STARTED

Consultant:	"Hi. I'm Mary Jones. You're Stan Martin?"
Interviewee:	"Yes. Come in. I've been expecting you, Ms. Jones. Any trouble getting to my out-of-the-way corner?"
C:	"No. Your receptionist downstairs has obviously guided lots of visitors here. She knew all the turns. For no windows, you've done a lot to fix this office up nicely."
I:	"Thank you. It took my wife's good taste in drapes. Why don't you have a seat there on the couch, Ms. Jones. Would you like some coffee?"
C:	"No thanks, I'm all coffeed out, but please go ahead. And call me Mary."
I:	"OK, Mary. I'll have tea from my secret larder. Being this far away from things, I've rigged up my own snack bar."
C:	"Mr. Martin—"
I:	"Stan, please."
C:	"Stan, as you know our firm, Resource Planning Associates, has been retained by Oliver Door to review with you and other key people ways of increasing the long term growth and profitability of the company. This morning I'd like to take about an hour and a half to discuss with you first your position and organization in the company, and then some of your views on the problems and opportunities facing Oliver and particularly your ideas about increasing profitability and getting some new products on the market over the next few years. Lets begin with your position here and your major responsibilities."

Interviewee:	"Well, as you know, I'm the company Controller. I've been in this job for four years now, after starting as Assistant Controller five years ago."
Consultant:	"Umm. Good for you. Was that promotion planned when you came aboard, or did it just work out that way?"
I:	"I'm not really sure. I know when my boss quit to join another company, he recommended me for the job. Maybe he had that in mind when he hired me."
C:	"Well, you didn't disappoint him. What are the major functions you cover?"
I:	"I have all the accounting, of course, and our computer group. I've added financial analysis and forecasting over the last three years. I have four people in that area now."
C:	"Sounds like a useful addition. How did that come about?"
I:	"Well, I felt we were always flying blind around here when it came to predicting cash needs, and no one really seemed to know what profit we were making on each product line. Now we know our costs, by product, and our budgets seem to be getting more accurate every year—knock on wood."
C:	(Laugh)"Maybe in another 50 years . . . Seriously, that's quite an accomplishment. What other functions do you supervise?"

ETC.

Chapter 4

GUIDING AND CONTROLLING THE INTERVIEW

When the stage has been properly set and the interviewee launched on his first topic, the consultant's primary role is to direct the interview so that it produces a maximum of useful information within the approximate time frame allowed. To do this, the consultant uses a variety of comments and questions to guide and control the pace, subject matter, and quality or depth of material being covered.

TYPES OF COMMENTS AND QUESTIONS

The comments and questions used to guide and control the interview can be classified according to their purpose as follows:

28

To Get More Information

The most commonly used phrase in interviewing is, "Tell me a little more about . . . ," or, "Tell me a little bit about . . ." (Later in this chapter we'll take up the use of the words, "a little" to soften the more peremptory "Tell me about . . .")

This is the simplest and most direct way to indicate the subject area you wish the interviewee to explore or amplify. A more subtle, but equally effective technique, is the "echo" or reflected comment: "You say the scrap rate here has always been too high." Properly intoned—as a reflected statement, not as a question—this technique encourages the interviewee to expand on his last remark.

To Clarify or Explain

Sometimes the interviewee will assume the consultant knows about a situation, event, or technology which plays an important role in his narrative. If the consultant does not or is not sure, he should interrupt and ask for clarification: "What did you mean by 'the September Massacre' layoff?" Or, for explanation: "What role does limestone play in fluidized bed combustion systems?" Reasonable homework will prepare the consultant to deal with the major industry issues, the general company background, and some of the specialized terminology which characterizes most businesses. The consultant cannot be expected to know everything. An honest admission of ignorance is preferable to being caught trying to wing it or guess at the meaning of what is being said. Furthermore, most interviewees will be happy, even flattered, to be asked for an explanation of how their product works. On more than one occasion, such a probe has revealed a significant problem when the interviewee has admitted, "To tell you the truth, I really don't know how my bonus is figured out!"

A consultant shows his intelligence by his alertness and perceptiveness in handling the interview—not by what he knows about a particular industry, company or product. So ask away, especially early in the engagement.

The consultant who is still in the dark after two or three dozen interviews may well be regarded as slow, if not worse—incompetent.

To Corroborate Information

Frequently a consultant will want evidence to support an interviewee's statement. He may want such corroboration in order to pinpoint the sources of a problem, provide authority for a viewpoint, or elucidate an issue. In doing this it is important that the consultant avoid any implication that he doubts the client's word or is challenging his statement. (Challenging is a special problem which is dealt with in Chapter 7.) Therefore, a positive approach should be maintained, as in, "That's a very interesting idea you've come up with. Can you take me through some of the steps that led you to that conclusion?" Or, "I'd like to spend a minute or two exploring that viewpoint. Let's begin with some of the events or facts that convinced you and others that the company's policy was misguided there." Said in a supportive tone, these approaches avoid the mildly curious, "Why do you say that?"—or the more threatening, "Can you prove that?" These questions are too blunt and risk interrupting the cooperative and spontaneous flow of information the consultant has worked so carefully to induce.

To Remind the Interviewee Who Wanders

Sometimes we all get carried away. This can easily happen when the consultant has created such a supportive atmosphere and shows a strong interest in the interviewee's job, his opinions, accomplishments, and so on. So, to maintain control, the consultant needs to bring his client gently back on track by a summary comment and a reminder statement or question, e.g. "That certainly was a messy situation. Let's talk a little bit about the second problem you mentioned, poor cash controls." Or, "I can appreciate the frustration your team must have felt when all that work went down the drain. Getting back to planning, what was the employee reaction when the company announced its five year plan?"

To Move the Interview Along

This same summary/reminder approach is ideally suited to guide the interview along from topic to topic. For example, when the consultant feels that he has adequately explored the interviewee's major responsibilities he should conclude this topic by, "That gives me a good picture of your position and duties here. Let's talk next about your organization— whom you report to, who reports to you, and some of the thinking that went into your present structure."

It is important to milk each topic dry before moving on to the next. Otherwise, the consultant is always having to go back to various topics for things he missed, producing a very messy set of notes. On the other hand, time constraints require that the consultant move the interviewee along to the next topic when, in his judgement, the major findings have been unearthed. Arriving at this balance between time and substance takes both experience and a sense of when each interviewee has been drained of all essential information.

To Clarify the Consultant's Question

Sometimes interviewees get confused about what the consultant is seeking. Perhaps he has asked a Foreman to enumerate his problems. The Foreman hesitates, looking flustered. He's not sure whether you mean his personal problems, his problems on the job, the company's problems, or what. Here a laundry list question can clarify the interviewer's meaning or break a silence due to uncertainty about where to start. For instance, regarding the Foreman's problems, the consultant can say, "Is it finding qualified machinists, getting maintenance help when you need it, too much paper work—or what?" This laundry list offers a sufficient spread of options to pinpoint the type of problems the consultant is after. The "or what" at the end opens the door to other problems of this kind in case the interviewee doesn't wish to select one from the list offered.

Leading Questions

Leading questions are generally inappropriate for diagnostic interviews. The consultant is exploring for information, not suggesting views or conclusions to the interviewee. Therefore, unless the consultant has established
the groundwork, a question such as, "When did turnover
in your department become excessive?" can be upsetting
or even threatening. In turn, this puts the interviewee on
the defensive and disrupts the spontaneous flow.

An interesting type of leading question is explained
by Richardson, Dohrwend and Klein in their book, *Interviewing: Its Forms and Functions.** They illustrate the use of
a leading statement or question to provoke agreement or
denial. For our purposes, the consultant might say, "Most
Foremen tend to be autocratic, wouldn't you say?" The
interviewee may (1) agree, and go on to elaborate on this
as the only way to get the work out, or, as one of the
problems to be overcome in this plant; or (2) disagree, and
point out that this is *not* the case in this situation and
indicate other causes for employee unrest. Obviously, this
tactic should be used sparingly to avoid suspicion on the
part of the interviewee that the consultant is trying to trap
him—or that the consultant is a highly opinionated fool!

PROBING

Sooner or later the interviewee will bring up a subject or
situation which touches on a key issue or which may lead
to the heart of a problem. It may be a change in management policy, the firing of a key executive, or a comment
which supports or refutes one of the interviewer's hypotheses. When this happens, the consultant needs to investigate more deeply. He does this by probing to find out
what specifically happened, how it happened, why, who
was involved, and/or what resulted. Ideally, the interviewee will cover much of this material in his own way.
However, he may omit salient points, and it is up to the

* Basic Books, New York, 1965.

consultant to interrupt and dig in if he senses that the interviewee is moving on to other subjects.

THE GEIGER COUNTER

Richard Fear in his book, *The Evaluation Interview*, uses the analogy of a Geiger counter to illustrate how the interviewer decides when to probe for pay dirt. A passing comment on low morale or the lack of sufficient inspectors in the plant should start one's Geiger counter clicking, and indicate the need to dig in for more information.

Sometimes it's hard to know where to start digging. Take an example from the first topic the consultant is likely to cover, the interviewee's position in the company. Suppose the interviewee, responding appropriately to the consultant's encouragement, tells the following story:

> "When I took over this job two years ago, the place was a mess. Since then I've cleaned out the incompetents and troublemakers, recruited better talent, and fixed our problems. Today we are 22% ahead on productivity."

Such a statement raises a host of possible areas to probe. Is this guy a ruthless tyrant or a very effective leader? Just what was the nature of the mess and how deeply did he analyze it before he cleaned house? How does he assess talent? Can he rescue people or does he just replace them? Did the company assist him or was this all his own doing? Is a 22% improvement in productivity reasonable or should it have been 50%? How much improvement was due to people changes *vs.* better machinery, new systems, or other problems fixed.

Given this statement, the consultant's first response should be a pat, "That's quite an accomplishment," followed immediately by, "Tell me more about how you were able to do all of that," or, "I'd be interested in learning more about the mess you inherited and the specific steps you took to clean it up." These responses tell the interviewee that (1) you are impressed, and (2) you want more details. Further probes can be made as he covers the specifics of his story. The only caveat, as Fear points out, is that too many probes in quick succession can have the effect of converting a good flow of spontaneous information into a question/answer type of interview. If this should happen, that is, if the interviewee stops after each answer and waits for the next question, the consultant will have to prime the pump all over again to regain the spontaneous flow. This will require a conscious break in the question/answer pattern and a fresh approach to the next topic. For example, "That gives me a very clear picture of how you've been able to improve things here. Next, I'd like you to tell me about your organization—whom you report to, who reports to you, and how your organization evolved to its present form." If the consultant then sits back, waits expectantly, and injects early encouragers ("Uh-huh," "very interesting," etc.) and nods occasionally, the interviewee should resume his earlier pattern of spontaneous discourse.

SOFTENING PROBES IN SENSITIVE AREAS

Client personnel may be understandably reluctant to discuss information which could be self-incriminating, damaging to their department or company image, or highly confidential. They also may avoid comments which are derogatory toward their fellow employees or upper management if they are afraid such remarks will be reported and embarrass them—or worse, get them fired. Yet it may be vital to the engagement to get at the true causes of problems and the core issues however damaging or sensitive these may be.

In order to get at such sensitive information, the consultant can do several things. (1) He can establish an atmosphere of openness and trust by the manner in which he conducts the interview. As indicated in Chapter 3, most interviewees will respond spontaneously and candidly to friendlines, interest, receptivity, and encouragement. The consultant should establish this atmosphere early in the interview before he touches on or probes into sensitive areas. (2) The consultant can offer assurances of confidentiality if he is asked to, or if it is obvious that the interviewee is becoming ill at ease or doubtful about continuing along an embarrassing train of thought. (3) The consultant can soften his approach, thereby making it easier for the interviewee to disclose or discuss sensitive subjects and even his own mistakes.

The psychology of softening is intuitively understood by people who are sensitive to the feelings of others. It involves the use of one or more of the following five techniques.

Tentativeness

Some words and phrases have a tentative, even hesitant connotation which conveys to the interviewee a gentle or tactful approach to sensitive subjects. These words and phrases are:

might

perhaps

would you say that . . .

is it possible that . . .

. . . or not so much so

An example of this tentative phrasing technique would be, "*Is it possible that* top management *might* put in a little more time on planning?" How much more gently such a question strikes the listener than, "Are top managers bad planners?" Another example: "*Would you say that* selling expense in this office is somewhat high, *or not so much so?*" Again, a much easier discussion starter than, "Why are selling expenses so high?" (Note that the phrase, "or not so much so," offers the interviewee a choice of positions, either of which can be followed up by the consultant.)

Minimizing

Making light of a subject in the sense of moderating, deemphasizing or mitigating is a second techique for softening.

This involves using the following words and phrases:

a little bit

to some extent

some

somewhat

fairly

rather

An example here would be (combined with a tentative opener), *"Would you say that* the performance standards here were *somewhat* inconsistent?" This probe might follow a comment or indication by the interviewee that part of the company's problem was due to inconsistent appraisal and pay practices on the part of supervisors. If the interviewee answers that the performance standards are satisfactory, then the next logical probe would be, "Then what *might* account for *some* of the situations you have described?"

Face Saving

Certain phrases have a softening effect because they offer a psychological "out" or face saving escape from blame. Like Flip Wilson's Geraldine, most of us would like to excuse our mistakes by saying, "The devil made me do it!" The consultant can use this same psychology by employing the following phrases:

what might have accounted for . . .

what prompted your decision to . . .

how did you happen to . . .

has there been any opportunity to . . .

These phrases soften the otherwise too blunt and potentially pejorative, "Why did you . . ." (overrun the budget, miss an opportunity, allow a problem to continue, etc.). Following is an example (again combined with other softeners): *"Has there been any opportunity to* improve productivity *a little bit* over the past year?" If the answer is, "No," due to work pressures, a tight budget, too much paper work, and so on, the consultant must draw his own conclusions as to whether these are legitimate excuses or just rationalizations for lack of attention to a critical goal area. In either case, he has made it easier for the interviewee to admit to a potential shortcoming by suggesting that "lack of opportunity" was the culprit.

Indirection

Perhaps the most tactful method of dealing with sensitive or potentially embarrassing subjects is by indirection. For example, to get at such touchy topics as poor morale, indecisive management, inter-department frictions or a punitive atmosphere, the consultant can introduce the subject in a roundabout way. He may say, "Let's talk *a little bit* about factors which *might* influence morale around here— reward systems, opportunities to participate in decisions, management style, and the like. How would you rate these and similar factors?" (Note the use of softeners and the laundry list to get the interviewee started in the desired direction.) Another example: "Let's talk about management style at the XYZ Company, *Would you say* it was *somewhat* autocratic, *or not so much so?"* (Again note how the phrase, "or not so much so," gently nudges the interviewee one way or the other on this subject.)

The Balance Sheet Approach

Still another softening technique is the balance sheet or "good things/bad things" approach. This technique makes it psychologically easier to admit one's own or the company's shortcomings. Here the consultant asks the interviewee to analyze a department, a decision, a product or the boss by listing the strong points or assets, and also "things that *might* be improved *a little bit."* As the assets are brought out, each one is seconded or "patted" whenever possible. For example, "Yes, I certainly agree you are centrally located for your market;" "A strong decisive CEO is an asset to any organization;" and so on. These acknowledgements show that the consultant has an appreciation of the good things about the company or its people before delving into the bad things. If pursued long enough, and if the consultant can add a point or two along the way

("I've heard good things about your products back where I come from;" "It occurs to me your image in the market is a real plus;" etc.), the interviewee can become anxious to correct any impression that the company and its people are perfect. After all, everyone has problems. At the least this emphasis on the good things creates a more comfortable framework for confessing to some faults—"things one could improve on a little bit." (E.g., "Well, maybe the boss does get a little set in his ways now and then.")

As stated earlier, tactful and sensitive people will intuitively soften their approach in potentially touchy areas of the interview. With training and practice, anyone can learn to do this easily without thinking about it or fumbling for words. The occasions for using softening techniques are: (1) when dealing with sensitive subjects (if necessary, new interviewers should identify likely topics in advance); (2) early in the interview when assessing the sensitivity, objectivity and confidence level of the interviewee; (3) when the interviewee has been identified as a touchy type requiring careful handling; (4) whenever the interviewee shows signs of discomfort or embarrassment; and (5) when in doubt.

If the consultant has identified the interviewee as objective, cooperative, confident, and outspoken, he may proceed to question and probe in a direct manner without regard to softening techniques. He should be aware, however, that even the toughest may have a sore spot or two, and a somewhat softened approach is never wrong or in bad taste.

ENDING THE INTERVIEW

When the consultant has covered his topics as planned, including the follow up questions in each area (and any facts or views he feels he must challenge—see Chapter 7), he should bring the interview to a close by saying, "I see our time is up;" or, "Well, this has been a very helpful discussion;" or, "That gives me a good fix on several of the problems we have discussed;" or, some other phrasing which clearly signals the end of the meeting. Standing up, shaking hands and thanking the interviewee for his help complete the amenities, and, hopefully, leave the relationship on a friendly basis. This makes it easier for the interview to be continued in person or by phone if either party has an afterthought or question.

Sometimes interviewees will use these last minutes to add a few confidential remarks. If important, the substance can be noted after leaving the room. If the interviewee has a great deal to get off his chest or wishes to question the consultant at length, a future date may have to be set so that the consultant can keep to his schedule.

CONCLUSION

One might think that using a non-directive approach with each of five or six topics would open the interview to many hours of rambling. And it is true that the pace and tempo of the interview depend to some extent on the intelligence, perceptiveness, and analytical ability of the interviewee. However, it is up to the interviewer to guide and control the interview so that it accomplishes its purpose, covers the critical issues, and concludes within the allotted time span. This is accomplished by proper stage setting at the outset, milking each area dry of critical information and then moving on, probing into rich pay dirt areas whenever the Geiger counter starts clicking, and terminating the interview with courtesy and appreciation for assistance rendered to the engagement. All of this guidance and control should be done unobtrusively and without stemming the spontaneous flow or disrupting the trusting and candid mood of the interviewee. New interviewers may need supervised practice to develop their skills to be able to accomplish this. Appendices B and C contain probing and softening drills on which the novice interviewer may practice. Appendix E presents a training format which can be used as often as necesary to prepare the beginning interviewer. However, like the father told his son about girls, one has to quit reading about them and start going out on dates to find out what they are really like. Live interviews with real clients are the best teachers.

Exhibit 2 illustrates probing and softening techniques in an interview context.

Exhibit 2

PROBING AND SOFTENING

Consultant:	"Charley, you mentioned earlier that your maintenance costs were running higher each year. Can you tell me a little more about that?"
Interviewee:	"It's mostly repairs. Our machines are old—like I've been telling headquarters for years."
C:	"You've told headquarters this before."
I:	"Oh, many times . . . Seems as if no one is listening."
C:	"They don't listen."
I:	"Guess not. I understand the money is there, but it goes to the corporate office. You see, our bonus is figured on ROI—and the boss is 62 . . ."
C:	"You think it's Sam's chance to make a few bucks before he retires?"
I:	"Now look—I'm not pointing the finger at Sam. Maybe its what corporate wants. Maybe you better forget that last remark."
C:	"Charley, it's not my role to point any fingers or name names. I'll bring it up only if a number of people feel the same way and it looks like a problem to be investigated."
I:	"Well, there's plenty of us here who think that's what's going on—whether they tell you or not."
C:	"OK, I'll be on the lookout. And I can appreciate that the subject of Sam's retirement may be a bit sensitive around here."

Interviewee:	"It sure is."
Consultant:	"Well, while we're on the subject, let's talk a little bit about Sam. He's put in a lot of good years here. I assume he has something going for him. What would you say were his strong points—things he does best?"
I:	"Well, he knows this plant like the back of his hand."
C:	"He certainly impressed me on the plant tour. What else?"
I:	"Most everybody here has been hired by him, and up 'till recently, we've set company records."
C:	"Yes, it certainly appears to be a well-qualified bunch."
I:	"He's gone to bat for us over the years—raises and all. Most of us owe him a good deal on that."
C:	"He seems to have generated lots of loyalty over the years."
I:	"And I guess you could say he's one of the best around when it comes to figures—costs and all."
C:	"That's an impressive list of talents."
I:	"On public relations, I'd have to give him a mixed rating. Some like him. Others can't stand him."
C:	"Yes, I can see that. What about communications?"
I:	"Well, upward I guess it's good. I know our division is well thought of, and performancewise we have maxed out on bonus for the past eight years. It's just that Sam's survivors will have to pay the price."
C:	"You mean lack of reinvestment over the years will have to be made up?"
I:	"Yes—and in my opinion we're overdue."
C:	"Maybe Sam just can't be objective about these things so near retirement."

Interviewee:	"Several of us feel that way. Maybe your engagement can come up with some investment proposals."
Consultant:	"What about other areas—is Sam OK regarding giving raises, training staff, hiring good people lately?"
I:	"No. In fact, now that you mention it, he seems to have slacked off on all that sort of thing lately. He doesn't even want to talk with us much these days."
C:	"So it's a general pattern. Just old age, or what?"
I:	"I don't know."
C:	"Any ideas about how we might fix things? Just specifying some investment dollars may not do it if Sam can sabotage the deal."
I:	"I don't know. Maybe another assignment for Sam in the company—maybe Vice President of National Accounts. I understand that's a job they're thinking about upstairs."
C:	"In other words, get Sam away from here."
I:	"Yeah—or get the business away from Sam."
C:	"How might that be done?"
I:	"Make our Product Managers into General Managers, with Sam out of the day-to-day operations."
C:	"Sounds like an interesting idea. Tell me how that might work."

ETC.

Chapter 5

LISTENING AND RECORDING INFORMATION

BARRIERS TO COMMUNICATIONS

We all start out thinking that listening comes naturally. We seem to be doing it every waking hour of our lives. In the last half century, however, many studies have shown that the communication process is fraught with perils. Wendell Johnson's article on *The Fateful Process of Mr. A Talking to Mr. B.** lists the physiological hazards of the process: the limitations of our sensory receptors; the preconditioning of our "filter" system; the problems of translating symbols or ideas into words using our own peculiar vocabulary; the distractions and "static" inherent in the environment and air waves through which our conversation is transmitted;

---

* Reprinted from the *Harvard Business Review* in *On Human Relations*, Harper & Row, New York, 1979.

and, finally, a parallel set of hazards within the receiver's makeup like those within the sender.

To these physiological barriers to communication, speech professor Irving Lee* lists three attitudinal obstacles:

1. Mr. A assumes that Mr. B uses words just as he does
2. Mr. A assumes that unless Mr. B feels as he does, he is a fool, and
3. When Mr. B talks, he likes to get things off his chest which may not be directly related to the subject or purpose Mr. A has in mind.

More recently, a number of studies have been conducted on "body language," some of which suggest that people communicate more, or more reliably, by their nonverbal behavior than by what they say. Frequently, dress, posture, gestures, and facial expression combine in behavioral clusters to portray various psychological states such as openness, defensiveness, enthusiasm, doubt, boredom, tension, and so on. Even lying may be telegraphed by such gestures as shaded eyes or pulling on an ear lobe.

It is important for a consultant to be aware of both barriers and aids to communication. For starters, he should know himself well enough to understand his own biases and make allowances for these. J. Krishnamurti observed, ". . . most of us listen through a screen of resistance. We are screened with prejudices, whether religious or spiritual, psychological or scientific; or with our daily worries, desires, and fears . . . Therefore, we listen really to our own noise, to our own sound, not to what is being said."**

In my experience, while consultants suffer from the usual array of blind spots and prejudices, they are particularly susceptible to intellectual conceit. They tend to agree with Puck's sentiments in *A Midsummer-Night's Dream*, "What fools these mortals be!" This viewpoint stems primarily from repeated exposure to client problems, some of which

---

* From *How to Talk with People*, Harper & Bros., New York, 1952.
** *The First and Last Personal Freedom*, Harper & Bros., N.Y., 1954.

must seem to outsiders to be self-induced and indeed foolish. Like some psychoanalysts who see patients all day and tend to view the world as made up primarily of neurotics, consultants can become supercilious about their clients. This is an attitude which will show through if not controlled—or, better yet, understood and dispelled.

LISTENING TO FEELINGS

Consultants must obviously listen for facts. Equally importantly, however, they must also listen with a "third ear." This means listening not only to what is being said but also to the underlying feelings of the interviewee. In their textbook, *Personnel*,* authors Strauss and Sayles discuss interview techniques. They point out that responding to the interviewee's emotional message can open the way to a fuller exploration of complex and even highly sensitive areas. They cite as an example the employee who blurts out, "The reason I want to quit is that so-and-so foreman keeps pestering me. He won't give me a chance!" On hearing such a statement the consultant's Geiger counter should start clicking. He should dig in to find out what is going on, but without further upsetting the interviewee who may feel he has already said too much. If the consultant says, "Where would you go if you quit?" or, "What are you doing that might make him pester you?" he either sidetracks the discussion or concedes that the foreman may be right. In either case he has failed to respond to the interviewee's need to air a grievance. He may also have missed a chance to get at a key problem which is disrupting shop operations. Instead, the consultant's more perceptive response should reflect the interviewee's most central feeling, for example, "He won't give you a chance?" This response encourages the interviewee to tell the rest of the story without committing the consultant to side with either the foreman or the subordinate. It also probes for pay dirt regarding supervisory practices on the shop floor.

* Prentice-Hall, Inc. Englewood Cliffs, N. J., 1967.

Appendix D presents a number of drills to improve interviewers' empathetic listening skills.

RECORDING INTERVIEWS

After a day of interviews, the best of listeners will be confused if he cannot capture and retain the facts, perceptions, and conclusions arrived at during each interview. There are several commonly used methods for capturing and retaining interview content. These are discussed as follows:

Tape Recording

Tape recorders have obvious and significant advantages. When they function properly, they are the most comprehensive and accurate means of capturing everything that is said.

However, tape recorders do have limitations. Unless they are also video-recorders, they do not include the body language or facial expressions which are often essential to a proper understanding of the speaker's feelings and intent. Second, when a tape is rolling, the consultant may get careless about detail, feeling confident that the recorder is getting it all. Of course, it can't pick up the details which the consultant forgets to elicit.

Third, some interviewees are awkward or become nervous when they are being recorded. While a skilled interviewer can overcome this distraction, the recorder's presence can become noticeable at any time, especially when the tape must be turned or changed.

Fourth, according to Murphy's Law, things go awry with electro-mechanical devices: batteries need changing; the recorder runs out of tape; you forget to start it; etc.

Perhaps the biggest problem in the use of tape recorders, however, is that for most engagements they are inefficient. The consultant usually ends up listening to the same interview more than once, and may even save note taking for the second time around!

Post-Interview Note Taking

Some consultants cannot take notes while they interview. Many beginners find it hard to concentrate on interview techniques while taking notes. In either case, it is essential that time be allowed after each interview to write down highlights, significant facts, and key perceptions. This may take 10–20 minutes, depending on the amount of material covered. Sad experience has shown that failure to write up each interview immediately after it is concluded results in an impossible confusion of facts and impressions at the end of a day of interviewing.

Note Taking During the Interview

The optimum approach to recording interview data is to take notes while the interview is in progress. The advantages of this method are, (1) it is efficient since it can capture all key elements the first time through, (2) it enables the interviewer to record both data and impressions, both facts and feelings as these emerge in the discussion, and (3) when interviews are properly planned, notes can be arranged for easy retrievability and comparison. That is, all interviews lead off with the interviewee's major responsibilities, followed by organization analysis, company or department assets, problem issues, or whatever pattern was established at the outset of the engagement. This orderly approach to data collection greatly simplifies the subsequent task of analysis, even when teams of interviewers are involved in very large engagements.

Because of its many advantages, I would urge beginners to start off taking notes during their interviews and allow a few minutes after each interview to adjust them, add key words, quotes, etc. (Even experienced consultants need to do this after particularly fast paced or pregnant interviews.) Since most consultants today are college graduates, many with MBAs, they have spent many hours taking notes during classroom lectures. In this process, they have developed some shorthand code to speed them along. "Businessese" also helps by providing hundreds of conventionally accepted abbreviations (CEO, MIS, OD, R&D, etc.), to which each of us can add his own.

While some details may be missed, it is unlikely that major points will escape even the novice note taker. With time, practice, and experience, the consultant will develop high confidence in his notes as the most important input to his findings, analysis, and recommendations.

MECHANICS

A few suggestions should be added here about the mechanics of note taking.

- Note pads should be held unobtrusively on one's knees or lap. If placed on the desk or table top they can be distracting to the interviewee. Also, a surprising number of people have learned to read upside down, and curiosity about what the consultant is putting down can be overwhelming. This positioning of one's note pad also makes page turning less noticeable, thereby keeping the interviewee's attention on the consultant and not on his notes.

- Pens or pencils should be held at the ready when not in use. Putting them down and picking them up is not only distracting, it signals to the interviewee which of his statements the consultant considers noteworthy and which he chooses to ignore. This is a game one does not wish to play with interviewees.

- Good eye contact is essential throughout the interview. Therefore, the consultant must avoid burying his head in his notes. While a few consultants have mastered the art of "blindfold" writing, I have found that glancing at one's notes—even if done frequently— need not disrupt the interviewee's impression of continuous eye contact. I recall a client remark after a two-hour interview: "You will have a tough time remembering all we have talked about." He was completely unaware that I had taken over twenty pages of notes during our discussion.

- Writing down "good news" as it emerges is fine. However, when "bad news" is being discussed, it is preferable to avoid note taking, especially if the subject may be embarrassing to the interviewee. On these occasions, defer note taking until the discussion moves on to other topics and then record the sensitive information. Any movement to immediately record damaging data can quickly put an interviewee on the defensive.

- Consultants should develop some standard format for their notes. In Chapter 2 a shorthand acronym was suggested for remembering the sequence of interview topics. (E.g., ROGAPI for Responsibilities, Organization, Goals, Assets, Problems and Ideas for solutions.) These reminder letters can be placed at the head of one's notepad, on each page, or on a side memorandum—wherever they are most handy when needed. This ordering of topics makes it easier to locate common themes when compiling the results of many interviews.

- Finally, I suggest that the novice consultant divide each page of his notes to record impressions, ideas and judgments on the left hand 1/3rd of the page, and facts, narrative and evidence on the right hand 2/3rds of the page. Exhibit 3 illustrates this technique. In a way, this format emphasizes the two kinds of listening discussed earlier in this chapter—listening empathetically and listening for facts. When analyzing such notes it is easy to pinpoint on the right hand part of the page the facts or evidence which gave rise to the consultant's opinions recorded on the left hand side of the page.

CONCLUSION

Listening and note taking or recording, like interviewing, are essential consulting skills. They must be exercised on virtually every engagement. It is true that these skills cannot substitute for sound judgment in solving client problems, but good judgments regarding a client's needs require a solid foundation of comprehensive and accurate findings, elicited by perceptive listeners, and carefully recorded for analysis.

Exhibit 3

NOTE TAKING

Has moved up well	Started 12 yrs. ago as clerk. Supv. in 2 yrs.—Asst. Mgr. in 5 yrs. Mgr. in 8 yrs.
Ambitious, tries hard	Wants VP Sales—going to nite sch. for MBA. Needs 2 more yrs. Now supv. 16–17 as Mgr. Inside Sales incl. order dept., drafting, est., pricing & cust. svce.
Not good on numbers	Pricing done by formula—Prod. Mgrs. do this. Don't know how. Engrs. set std. costs + mfg. input.
Picks good talent Can he devel. any from within? Not a delegator Mother hen type	Has 4 supvs—all picked from outside. Inherited older group of employees—hi paid, knowledgeable, but set in their ways. "I do it better than my people"—often stays late to "clean up" (bachelor, job is his life!)
No way! Why so blind here?	Sam Bailey is backup. Age 39. Knows job. Does what I tell him. Only prob.—too soft on subords. I'll coach him on this.
Speaks his mind—why ineffective with boss, peers?	Probs: (1) Mfg. dominates our bus. They run what they want to look good. Sales could fix, but won't speak up.

Has ideas—but "up from office boy" prob. in impacting on bosses.

(2) QC is poor. $90K paid out in warranties last year.

(3) We over-engr. our product. Should design for "adequacy" not Cadillac of the industry.

Blames everyone else for Co. probs. How about CEO—why doesn't he see probs. & fix?

(4) Unions get away with murder. We're soft. Pers. Dept. gives in on negotiation and grievances. E.g., Absentee fired—then reinstated with back pay.

Some real org. confusion here!

Reports to Pres. *and* V.P. Sales, depending on subject or decision area!

ETC.

Chapter 6

INTERPRETATION

Interpretation is the payoff phase of an engagement. It distills the data collected on site, observed, and captured during interviews. It analyzes and evaluates them, and produces the conclusions and recommendations which will solve the client's problems or achieve the purpose of the engagement. By knowing what will be involved in the interpretation phase of an engagement, the consultant can properly plan his interview topics and follow up questions to obtain the findings necessary to prove or disprove his hypotheses.

Interpretation is the result of a complex mental process which includes:

- the compilation of facts, statements, observations, events, and impressions gleaned during the data gathering phase of the engagement
- analysis or the application of reasoning to the classification of data and the search for cause-effect relationships; and
- evaluation of all the above in the light of the consultant's experience, training, special insights, and wisdom.

COMPILATION

Inputs to compilation come from all forms of data gathering: materials, surveys, interviews, observations, and inferences. The last may be defined as impressions derived from a series of hints or clues, all pointing in the same direction—similar to circumstantial evidence in a criminal investigation. For example, the need for product managers might emerge from: poor communication between functional departments, lack of product cost or profit numbers, lack of product development goals, general *vs.* pinpointed product advertising, poor product knowledge among field salespeople, and so on.

Regarding the compilation of interview notes, three different problems may arise: (1) interviewees sometimes shade their stories or lie, (2) interviewees present conflicting views or "facts", and, (3) arranging data may be difficult due to poor note-taking or the large volume of information generated by big engagements.

Is He Telling the Truth?

An early and sometimes continuous task in every interview is to determine whether the interviewee is telling the truth. Many motives prompt an interviewee to warp the truth or tell out-and-out lies. Their own job security or career future may be on the line. They may feel they must protect a friend, their boss, or their department. They may resent the intrusion of the consultants and try to lead them astray. Or, they may wish to appear more knowledgeable than they are and fabricate or assume facts/events they don't know about.

It is important that the consultant be aware of such motives and alert to the following indicators of honesty or dishonesty.

- Admissions of error or poor judgment are usually characteristic of people who are being open and above board.

- Internal consistency of the interviewee's story provides another clue. Does it hang together and make sense? Are the events and results plausible? Are the causes sufficient for the outcomes produced? For example, was a general strike by all employees likely because a supervisor disciplined a clerk for smoking, or isn't it more likely that far more pervasive and deep seated problems were already present?

- Is it likely that the interviewee would know, understand, or have access to the information he is relating? If not, was his source a reliable informant?

- Body language will sometimes unmask exaggeration or lying. The interviewee may hem and haw, blush, or squirm in his seat. Some writers on body language maintain that the three monkeys—see no evil, hear no evil, speak no evil—symbolize three clues to deception: (1) avoiding eye contact or shading one's eyes with his hand, (2) tugging at an ear lobe, and, (3) covering one's mouth while speaking. (Much depends on the context here. Maybe the interviewee just has an itchy ear lobe!)

- Other likely giveaways are attempts to change the subject or skim rapidly over potentially significant material.

The times to be most alert for deception or bias are when the interviewee is discussing events which can enhance or detract from his own image or role. On these occasions, if the interviewer suspects that the interviewee is exaggerating or lying, he should not challenge the interviewee or disrupt the spontaneous flow of discourse. A probe or two will tell whether the interviewee is going to stick to his story or back off, claiming he misspoke or was misunderstood. If the consultant wishes to challenge the interviewee, he should do so at the end of the interview when he has little to lose. (See Chapter 7 on how to challenge.)

Conflicting Views

Like the blind men feeling the elephant, we see events and situations from our own point of view, and most engagements involve at least some differences of this kind. These differences may not be due to intended deception. Honest men may differ due to different perspectives, judgments, and perceptions. In such situations the consultant should first seek external evidence or objective criteria to resolve the differences in his mind. Failing this, he must use his own best judgment regarding (1) the most plausible story, and/or (2) the most honest and open interviewees.

The frequency of conflicting views teaches the experienced consultant to avoid jumping to conclusions early in an engagement. Often at the end of the first day or two of interviews, it appears that the white hats are clearly identifiable and that the solution is obvious. Sometimes a single interview will seem to illuminate the whole situation with insightful perceptions and cogent answers to all the problems. Typically, however, as the engagement progresses, the plot thickens, the truth turns out to be somewhere between the white and black hats' positions. The solutions are neither obvious nor simple. This is why even the most seasoned consultants often find it advisable to confer with their peers, sleep on it, and use informal previews or trial balloons before settling on their best judgements in a complex engagement.

Digesting Notes

On large engagements involving many interviews, interpreting one's notes can become a complicated task. Consultants who are new to such engagements should first plan their interviews in an orderly way so that data and opinions on each topic can be easily found in the notes. (See Chapter 5 on note-taking.)

Furthermore, some technique must be used to array assets, problems, and possible solutions in a comprehensible and orderly way. For very large assignments, computers are ideal for collecting all data and opinions related to each topic in a retrievable manner. For smaller engagements, accountants' spread sheets or analysis pads are useful for compiling interviewee comments under topical headings.

ANALYSIS

The analytical process involves the separation of elements and their categorization or classification in such a way that judgments may be made and conclusions reached. For example, assets, problems, and ideas for solution can be arranged in order of seriousness, profit contribution, cost impact, function, department, and so on. The number of interviewees commenting on each item can be tallied to show the extent of awareness or concern. Problem solutions can be compared for cost and effectiveness.

Whatever compilation technique is used, the result should enable the consultant to (1) identify the major strengths or assets of the enterprise, (2) list and prioritize the significant problems to be solved, and, (3) compile, compare and evaluate the proposed solutions for each problem identified.

EVALUATION

The evaluation process is the heart of the consultant's contribution to an engagement. In addition to the quantitative aspects of the client's situation (pro forma projections, profit trends, the impact of layoffs, etc.) the evaluation process must deal with three qualitative considerations, as follows:

Degree

Judgments are not usually a matter of right or wrong, good *vs.* bad, but of how good or how bad. Is the problem life-threatening, or is it a mild infection that can be treated with reasonable care and standard remedies? Consultants often paint the bleakest picture in order to shake up the client, justify the solution proposed, and motivate implementation. These are legitimate tactics provided they are kept within the larger perspective of the client's overall state of health. Consultants who cry "wolf," lose credibility with sophisticated clients. The inclusion of assets to build on, along with problems to be fixed, helps to keep the consultant's analysis in balance.

Priorities

Once the problems have been listed, they need to be arranged in order of importance to the welfare of the client and the aims of the engagement. Problems which are easy and inexpensive to solve—even with high payoff—may not be critical to the client's major concerns. Consultants often earn their pay by properly arraying a client's problems, and bringing into focus the essential causes of difficulty or threats to the viability of the entire enterprise.

Practicability

A third issue of the evaluation phase relates to the adequacy of resources, time, and personnel to accomplish workable solutions. Will further studies be needed? Should more capital be raised? Is the CEO or department head capable of carrying out the recommendations? Are several stages needed to move the organization from here to there—and what tests and check points along the way will signal proceed, or stop and redirect the solution?

CONCLUSION

No consultant—or other professional—can reasonably be expected to be omniscient. He is, however, expected to observe due diligence: to do his homework, document his findir ;s, and give his best thought and judgment to the solu ns he proposes. In other words, he should be able to say *why* he recommends what he does—and defend his position. To do this well he must possess a number of essential consulting skills, among them critical thinking, problem solving, client presentations, and report writing.* However, the usefulness of all these skills, depends on a solid base of findings, including properly conducted interviews and an orderly set of notes which capture the salient points for later interpretation.

* Books and articles on these and other consulting topics can be obtained by contacting (1) ACME Inc. at 230 Park Ave. New York, N. Y. 10169; and, (2) the Consultants Bookstore, Templeton Road, Fitzwilliam, N. H. 03447.

Chapter 7

SPECIAL SITUATIONS

Anyone who does much interviewing will sooner or later meet up with a hostile interviewee. There may be someone who wants to interview the interviewer, or the boss who wants to know what each of his subordinates is saying about him. Some people intuitively handle these situations well. Others get flustered, confused, or even angry. A little preparation will enable the interviewer to handle such predicaments more adroitly, with a minimum of disruption to the interview process, or the client-consultant relationship. This chapter provides some suggestions for coping with some of these special situations.

CONFIDENTIALITY

When sensitive topics are obviously central to an engagement (e.g., the causes of losing major government contracts), the subject of confidentiality can be dealt with at the start of each interview. Otherwise, consultants should not bring up the issue of confidentiality. Like preaching on sin, it only gives people ideas. If the initial part of the interview has been well handled, the interviewer should

58

have established an atmosphere of openness and trust—
trust that the consultant will not use any information dis-
closed in a way that will undermine or damage the interviewee. To bring up this subject can break the spell and
sow doubt where there was trust. It goes without saying
that the consultant should live up to this trust. If client
personnel get fired, demoted, or otherwise damaged as a
result of the engagement, it should be because of their
generally known statements, documented performance
factors, or a reduction in force. It should not be the result
of comments made during the interview.

No matter how open and trusting the atmosphere the
consultant has created, however, during most engagements one or more interviewees will at some point bring
up the subject of confidentiality. This concern will be phrased
in a number of ways: "Who is going to read your notes?"
"Are you going to tell my boss?" "Can I tell you something
in confidence?" "I'm not sure I should be telling you all
this."

The consultant can handle confidentiality in one of
several ways, depending on the situation.

- At one extreme he can say, "Please don't tell me anything you don't want repeated to higher management." Or, "Consider everything you say to be on the
  record." If the engagement is highly sensitive or an
  adversary one, such as an unfriendly takeover situation, this kind of warning may be stated at the outset
  of the interview—sort of a Miranda-like warning. Or
  it may be inserted when a touchy subject comes up,
  e.g., the interviewee's role in safety rule infractions or
  a major cost overrun.

- A more flexible response would be, "I plan to combine
  your comments with others and present only the major
  or significant findings from all interviews to management—without indicating any single source." If the
  source would be obvious from the comments themselves, the consultant owes it to the interviewee to
  state that if his comments are vital to the engagement
  the consultant will use his best judgment regarding

how he will use them in his presentations to management.

- A third approach would be to agree, if the interviewee insists, that his comments will be kept in confidence. To reinforce this promise, the consultant should refrain from note-taking while a confidential subject is being discussed, For very shy or nervous types, the consultant may have to wait until the end of the interview, close up his note book, put away his pen, and lean forward in his chair to signal his readiness to discuss the most confidential matters.

The key issue regarding confidentiality is not which approach the consultant uses, but his integrity in abiding by his word. If he says he will keep the interviewee's comments in confidence then he should do so, bearing in mind that there are many ways to modify a comment or opinion, or disguise a source so that it cannot be identified.

A last word on confidentiality. In my experience it has often turned out that interviewees are eager to tell what they know or think regardless of the consultant's stand on confidentiality. They may even use the "off the record" prefix to underscore the importance of their remarks. After a pro forma concern over secrecy, they proceed to relate the most sensitive material. A common parallel in fact and fiction would be, "I promised Bill I'd never tell this to anyone—and I'll kill you if you repeat it, but . . ." Some things are just too juicy or important to be kept to oneself!

HOSTILITY

Handling hostility or an interviewee who refuses to talk or cooperate can be tricky. Inexperienced interviewers may need some rehearsal to deal with such situations in ways that do not further aggravate client personnel or disrupt the engagement. Following are a few general guidelines and some suggested steps which should restrain the hostility, and may even open up a balky interviewee and save the interview.

A basic rule of interviewing, and the first line of defense against balks, is to *assume consent*. For example, don't say, "Would it be all right if we begin with your job?" Or, "May we discuss your role in trying to keep costs down?" Instead say, "Let's begin by discussing your job," and, "I'd be interested in the success—or lack of it—of cost reduction programs in this company."

When, by silence or his demeanor, it is obvious that the interviewee is hostile, it is essential that the consultant remain calm and uninvolved in the hostility. Do not take it personally. Instead, let the interviewee vent his feelings while you try to understand what prompts them. Is it past experience with consultants, fear of layoffs, or concern that he or his department will be blamed for something? Or possibly it's his strong disagreement with management over the need for this engagement when he has been telling them all along what the problems are and what they must do to fix them.

If the consultant can reflect the interviewee's feelings, he can sometimes get at the source of the hostility and even rescue the interview. For example, he might try, "I can understand how you might feel about not wanting this project. I gather you feel that . . . , or did you have other reasons?" This response conveys understanding and acceptance of the interviewee (but not necessarily agreement with him), and probes for further sources of hostility.

When the interviewee has calmed down, the consultant might try, "Assuming you are right about that, what might be two or three solutions or improvements you would like to see around here?" This approach moves the interview quickly to the heart of the matter, and, after some judicious patting of the interviewee's ideas (e.g., "that sounds like a very interesting approach"), should calm the person sufficiently to go back to other topics the interviewer may want to cover before terminating the interview.

Sometimes consultants are warned in advance about a potentially hostile individual. If such hostility is immediately apparent, it can be confronted by, "I understand you have been dead set against this project from the start, Mr. Smith. However, since the Board has insisted, let's do the best we can. I'd be interested in getting your views on . . ."

As the above illustrations point out, interviewers should abandon the planned topical sequence when confronted by hostility. Anger or resentment must be dealt with first before other subjects can be discussed.

As a final point, consultants should be aware that some balks simply cannot be overcome. It is often impossible, for example, to force an interviewee to incriminate himself. Also, information which is obtained under duress is usually worthless or misleading. Therefore, if it becomes obvious to the consultant that the interviewee is hostile and has clammed up, he should follow these steps:

(1) Restate the question or topic, together with the reasons for wanting this information. E.g., "It is important for our study of productivity to get a clear picture of your organization and how the work flows from department to department. That's why I'd be interested in your reporting relationships and how you have structured your department.".

(2) If the interviewee still refuses to cooperate, the consultant should (a) acknowledge the reluctance ("I gather you don't want to talk about this now."), (b) stress the importance of his input ("We very much value your special perspective and views on this subject."), and, (c) disengage as gracefully as possible ("We don't want to put you on the spot. Let's drop it for today. If you change your mind, please let me know. Goodbye for now.")

(3) Report to his project leader or the client department head that he has encountered a balk. Ultimately, it is the client who must decide what to do about it, if anything.

FEEDBACKS TO DEPARTMENT HEADS

It is often helpful for the consultant to report back to each department head on the results of interviews with his subordinates. This practice:

- informs the department head of the consultant's findings without going over his head,
- permits clarification of questions, problems or misunderstandings, including corroboration or modification of significant findings,
- gives the department head an opportunity to point out corrective measures taken or planned so these may be included in the consultant's report, and,
- maintains the integrity of the consultant-client relationship at each level of the organization.

There are, however, some problems and caveats related to this procedure. It obviously shouldn't be done if expressly prohibited by the head of the client organization. The consultant may also wish to avoid such a feedback session if the department head is *THE* problem, or if there is a highly sensitive or adversary relationship between the consultant and the department head or client (e.g., an operational audit or consulting assignment to investigate widespread embezzlement or mismanagement at a subsidiary company).

Sometimes the consultant may decide that a face saving or perfunctory feedback is desirable, avoiding details, conclusions, or personnel evaluations. In this case he should be prepared to sidestep these issues as tactfully as possible. Here are some suggested replies to requests for details and/or conclusions:

- "I'll need some time to get my notes and thoughts together."
- "We plan to present you with all that after our team has met to compare notes and analyze all of our findings."
- "I'm on my way to a meeting now, but I'll get back to you on that as soon as I can get my report in order."

The objective of the face saving or perfunctory feedback is to present to the department head only the obvious highlights of the interviews—the assets or problem areas that he already knows about. This is done so that he feels informed and part of the engagement without getting embroiled in details, pressing for conclusions before they are ready, or upset prematurely over changes which may affect him or his department.

Many department heads want to know what the consultant thought about his key people or a particular individual. Unless this is included as an output of the engagement and the consultant is trained in evaluation techniques, he should be wary of engaging in personality assessments or psychoanalysis. Some suggested responses may be helpful in this area:

- As a general rule, the consultant should be tentative and very limited in his response: "I have only a few impressions. We weren't really checking on performance or trying to evaluate your people."
- Accentuate the positive: "Tom's explanation of the insurance claims department was most helpful."
- On negatives, stick to the obvious—what he already knows: "I can see what you meant about Bill. He does seem upset about his transfer."
- Some firms have a stated policy that consultants not discuss personnel with the client. This provides an easy out, or can be used to reinforce the response: "We really don't go into that aspect in our work."

CHALLENGING

To preserve the spontaneity of the interview, challenging should usually be done at the conclusion. At this point there is little to lose. Done earlier during the interview, challenges raise defenses and stop the unguarded and spontaneous flow of information. The major exception to this rule would be the case where the interviewee is obviously trying to make a fool of the consultant or lead him down the garden path. When this is suspected, the consultant might say, "Mr. Jones, our research on this engagement indicated that . . . Were we mistaken or how might this be explained?" This reply shows that the consultant has prepared himself in advance and will not be easily fooled. If the interviewee persists, a confrontation may be necessary: "You seem determined to mislead me, Mr. Jones. Are you concerned about this project, our findings, what we may tell your boss?"

Openly deceptive or hostile interviews can, of course, be truncated or aborted. However, they should not be abandoned without some attempt to unearth the causes of failure to cooperate. Such probing can sometimes reveal important findings: bad morale, a disgruntled employee, or even a conspiracy to head the project off in a false direction.

In the case of a routine challenge at the end of the interview, the consultant wishes to check an earlier statement to see if the interviewee will change his story, or whether the consultant's information was in error. In either case, a face saving approach is called for. For example: "Earlier, Mr. Smith, you mentioned that . . . The Annual Report, however, was quite specific about this matter. Can you clear up my misunderstanding on this?"

If the engagement objectives are to uncover facts and design a new or improved system, then getting the right information is critical. For this objective evidence is usually obtainable without challenging the interviewee. If the engagement objectives are, or include, getting an evaluation of people, morale, attitudes, and the like, then challenging may be important to discover why people may be motivated to color their statements or attempt to mislead the consultant. Otherwise, it is not the consultant's job to provoke client personnel, call them liars or challenge for the sake of challenging. The facts are what's important, and in some instances employees may honestly differ or be misinformed. Obviously, judgment and caution are needed where challenging is concerned.

INTERVIEW REVERSAL

Curiosity, anxiety or mischief may on rare occasions prompt the interviewee to try to become the interviewer. A few questions from the interviewee at the start of the interview can be expected. Some interviewees want to be sure they understand the situation, the agenda, or how and why your firm was selected for this engagement. Up to a point such questions are acceptable. However, if the questioning continues or lasts more than three or four minutes, the consultant should say, "That's a good question. I'll take some time at the end of the interview to cover that—and anything else I can clarify for you. But first I want to cover the information we need to complete our assignment. Let's begin with your position—the major responsibilities of your job."

Another approach might be, "I can see there's lots you want to discuss about our firm. Let's take time after we've finished our interview to cover any questions you may have. Now, let's begin with your position here—the major responsibilities of your job."

When the interview is over, the consultant can take a reasonable amount of time or schedule a special meeting if necessary to answer appropriate questions. This is time well spent if the interviewee is a senior executive or vital to the success of the engagement. In most cases, however, concerns about the qualifications of the consultant or his firm are put to rest by a thorough and professional interview.

USE OF FIRST NAMES

The issue of when to use first names usually resolves itself in most interpersonal encounters. This is also true in interviewing. As a general rule, if the consultant is young and the interviewee is (1) considerably older, (2) at a senior level, and/or (3) obviously reserved, formal or potentially hostile—the consultant should use Mr. or Ms. Miss or Mrs. is proper if she is introduced or generally known as such. If the interviewee begins using the consultant's first name, this is not necessarily a signal for the consultant to reciprocate. We've all seen White House press conferences where the President calls on a reporter by his/her first name, but they, in turn, reply with, "Mr. President."

Chapter 3 points out the importance of setting the proper stage to create trust and generate spontaneity. To initiate or presume intimacy can be considered rude by some people. The aim, as in the case of dress, manner and ice breaking, is to do the expected—and in this case respectful—thing. When in doubt, stick to Mr. and Ms. unless your intuition clearly says otherwise, or until the interviewee requests that you use his or her first name.

THE TEAM INTERVIEW

On large engagements it often saves time if several consultants interview the top executive or executives to gain an overall perspective on the client company. Usually, the consulting team will include the project head and two or three sub-group leaders. The advantage of the team interview approach is that all key members of the consulting firm get to hear the same story from the top management of the client company. The disadvantage is that the presence of several interviewers tends to reduce spontaneity and may, if not controlled, lead to a question/answer type of interview. To minimize this problem, the consulting group should select a lead interviewer who will conduct the entire interview. The other consultants present should take notes and wait until the conclusion of the interview to ask whatever questions they wish. Properly done, the interviewee will focus on the lead interviewer and become oblivious to the presence of the other people in the room.

This approach preserves as much spontaneity as possible in the situation, while still allowing each consultant present to ask any questions he has at the end of the pattern interview.

CONCLUSION

As stated at the outset of this book, interviewing is an extension and special application of one's natural interpersonal skills. In many cases, by 15 or 20 minutes into the interview the relationship will have developed into a comfortable, relaxed, and interesting exercise for both parties. The discussion will flow easily, questions don't need softening, key points can be probed and pinned down without concern for sensitivity or defensiveness. However, knowing the techniques for handling different kinds of people and some special situations will come in handy for any career consultant. No book can cover all the problem situations which can arise during interviews. In this chapter we have discussed only some of the more common ones. For the rest, one's common sense, intuition and a sense of humor are his best guides to an appropriate response.

Chapter 8

CONCLUSION

On the face of it, the consultant's role seems impossible. In a few weeks or months—sometimes in a few days—he is expected to gather data, diagnose the problems, and prescribe solutions for complex organizations, often employing hundreds and even thousands of people. In fact, there are three things which enable the consultant to do his job. They are:

(1) Virtually every assignment a consultant receives comes with some indication of where the difficulty lies— profits are down, sales are off, products are obsolete, good people don't stay, etc. Whatever the problem, the consultant has some function or issue on which to concentrate his attention. By scoping the project and doing his homework, he can often bring the problems into clear focus and identify a limited number of likely causes to investigate.

(2) If the consultant or his firm has been properly selected, he or they should bring to the engagement the special expertise required to analyze the client's problem in the light of similar problems in the pertinent industry, function or technology.

69

(3) Finally, using a diagnostic or pattern type of interview, the consultant can enlist the best minds, insights, and perhaps hundreds of man-years of experience to help him in his investigation. Also, this help comes from many levels and directions within the organization thereby surmounting the many barriers to communication which often blind companies to seeing themselves objectively. Properly conducted, this brain tapping should yield perceptive insights into the causes of all major problems, and provide a broad range of ideas for improvements and/or solutions to these problems.

This book has dealt primarily with the third of these three aids to effective consulting—the accessing of the best minds and thinking in the client organization by means of diagnostic interviewing.

To see ourselves as others see us is, as Robert Burns pointed out, a saving grace. It is also salutary for a company to see itself as its own employees see it—from many viewpoints and levels throughout the organization. Diagnostic interviewing enables the consultant to hold up this mirror to a client, reflecting back the collective perceptions of those with long and intimate association with the company and its problems. These perceptions, together with the consultant's focused investigation and special knowledge or wisdom make the consultant's role not only doable, but also essential for businesses in need of outside help.

APPENDICES

These appendices are composed of examples, drills, and practice exercises. They are intended for group training as well as individual use. Specialized consulting firms will obviously need to adapt or recreate the examples and exercises to fit their company's most typical engagements. However, the *types* of drills and exercises—designing a plan, probing, softening and reflecting feeling—are essential to developing skill in all forms of diagnostic interviewing. Even routine audits and implementation consulting require some diagnosis to assess the general competence of personnel, the client readiness for change, top management's support for programs or procedures, etc.

"Answers"—more exactly, "better responses" (there are no *best* answers)—are contained in Appendix F.

Appendix **A**

THE INTERVIEW PLAN

1. Sample Interview Plan
   a. Objective: To determine cause(s) of sales decline in the Western
         Region and develop solutions
   b. Interview Type: Pattern/structured plus Question/Answer
                   covering top management and Western Region
                   sales and administrative personnel
   c. Likely Causes (hypotheses):
      —weak/poor regional management
      —weak/poor regional sales force/distributors/reps.
      —emergence of strong regional/foreign competitor
      —lack of HQ support: skimpy advertising, slow delivery,
        misshipments, etc.
      —population/demographic/market shifts
      —changes in past year in regional policies, practices, personnel,
        organization, branch locations, pricing, training,
        compensation, quality, delivery patterns, communications,
        inventory levels, reorder procedures, etc.
   d. Topics to Cover:
      __4__ —Management/HQ support practices
(Topical __2__ —Organization and personnel policies, training,
sequence   competence, turnover, compensation, etc.

to be   _5_ —Problems—what has changed and why
used in   _3_ —Market(s)—description, composition, competitors
interview) _1_ —"Your position and major responsibilities"
               _6_ —Solutions and ideas for improvement
    e. Follow up Questions:
      Topic 1—how long in present job
            —training received
            —reports/comunications to HQ
            —authorities for pricing, hiring, local advertising/
              promotion
      Topic 2—layers of organization/communication problems
            —changes in past year
            —turnover, training, competence of sales force and
              support groups
            —pay/bonus/commission programs, benefits
      Topic 3—market share by branch
            —selling statistics—hit ratio, average sale, market
              coverage
            —what's our niche, special assets
            —what are our competitive disadvantages
      Topic 4—administrative controls and practices, sales reports,
              expense allowances, appraisal programs and
              effectiveness
            —policies regarding inventory levels, stocking of
              warehouses, quality, field service, warranties, delivery
              timeliness, technical assistance in the field, training
              budget, recruiting assistance, distributor/rep selection,
              volume discounts, pricing variances
            —competence of HQ and support personnel
            —investment in R&D, product improvement
            —investment in promotion, ads, packaging
      Topic 5—focus on problems to get at *root* causes versus
              symptoms
      Topic 6—cover all major problems indentified
            —is top management resistant to ideas and suggestions
              from the field?

    f. Lead Statement

      "As you know, Mr. Smith, Marketing Associates has been
      retained to assist management in analyzing and recommending

ways to improve sales in the Western Region. Today I'd like to take the next 2 hours or so to review with you your position, your organization, your market, how you see some of the problems at XYZ Corporation, and any ideas you may have on how the company can improve sales in this region."

  g. Lead Questions

     Topic 1—"Let's begin with your position—your major responsibilities."

     Topic 2—"Let's go on to organization—to whom you report, who reports to you, and how you have organized and manage your people."

     Topic 3—"I'd be interested in your views on XYZ's market and your place in it. Whom do you sell to, how do you sell, your competition, and any special assets or advantages your product has."

     Topic 4—"Incidentally, how about headquarters' role in your marketing efforts—how do they relate to you and what services or support do they provide?"

     Topic 5—"Let's summarize the major problem areas we have covered, and any we may have missed. I'd be interested in your analysis of some of the causes of these problems."

     Topic 6—"Let's conclude by getting your ideas about what it's going to take to fix some of these problems. Where do we begin?"

----

2. Practice in Forming Hypotheses and Selecting and Sequencing Topics

  a. Assume problem identified is *excessive turnover*. Likely causes might be: _____

_____

_____

_____

_____

_____

_____

_____

_____

Topics which would include these causes are:

Number
a proper
sequence)

— _____
— _____
— _____
— _____
— _____
— _____

Specific questions:
Topic 1_____
_____
_____
_____

Topic 2_____
_____
_____
_____

Topic 3_____
_____
_____
_____

Topic 4_____
_____
_____
_____

Topic 5_____
_____
_____
_____

Topic 6_____
_____
_____
_____

b. Assume problem identified is *excessive audit fees*. Likely causes might be:

_____
_____
_____
_____

Topics which would include these causes are:

(Number   —— _____
these in   —— _____
proper   —— _____
sequence) —— _____
           —— _____

Specific questions:

Topic 1_____

Topic 2_____

Topic 3_____

Topic 4_____

Topic 5_____

Topic 6_____

c. Assume problem identified is *manufacturing cost overruns.*
Identify likely causes, select and sequence topics, and write out:
Lead Statement

_____
_____
_____

Lead Questions

Topic 1—_____
_____

Topic 2—_____
_____

Topic 3—_____
_____

Topic 4—_____
_____

Topic 5—_____
_____

Topic 6—_____
_____

3. Select a typical engagement which you/your firm is likely to receive, and write up an interview plan covering:

Objective(s)
Type of interview you will use
Likely causes of the problem(s) i.e., hypotheses
Topics you will cover and sequence
Follow up questions for each topic
Lead Statement
Lead Questions for each topic

Appendix **B**

PROBING

Each of the following statements should set off your Geiger counter. You want to probe these in a way that gets at the key issue(s).

1. "People around here say it's Japanese imports that are killing our business, but I say it's bad management. We really ought to be much more profitable than we are."
   Your preferred response would be:
   a. "You feel the company should be more profitable."
   b. "Why is management so bad?"
   c. "Lots of people blame the Japanese."
   d. "That's an interesting idea. Tell me more."
   e. Say nothing—unless he changes the subject.
   f. Other: (write it out)

2. "John was a top engineer, but he couldn't get along with others. I finally told him off about it and he quit. Maybe I was wrong."
   Your preferred response would be:
   a. "What made John so good?"
   b. "I'm sure you had ample reason to get angry."
   c. Say nothing—unless he changes the subject.
   d. "You feel you might have been wrong?"
   e. "How else might you have handled the situation?"
   f. Other:

3. "I put Mary in charge of that department. She wasn't my best prospect, but I knew she'd quit if I put anyone else in charge."
   Write out your preferred response.

4. "Our data processing costs are doubling every 2 years. The DP Manager is a hell of a nice guy and seems competent, but if I even mention tightening up you'd think the world was going to stop!"
   Write out your preferred response.

5. "I joined this company because it was supposed to be well managed. But my R&D budget gets picked to pieces. Do they want new products around here or don't they? I wish they'd make up their minds. Maybe this project of yours will help them see my point."
   Write out your preferred response.

6. "Basically, this is a well managed plant—no matter what those guys in sales or engineering tell you."
   Write out your preferred response.

Appendix **C**

SOFTENING

Assume you want to soften the following probes in the ways indicated. Reword each question.

1. "Why did you overrun your capital budget this year?"
   a. Soften by face saving:

   b. Soften by indirection:

2. "Are you too soft on your people?"
   a. Soften by tentativeness and/or minimizing:

b. Soften by indirection:

c. Soften by a balance sheet type approach:

Reword the following probes so as to (a)soften their impact or pejorative connotation, and (b) encourage discussion of the subject *vs* a YES/NO/FACT type response.

3. "Forty people report to you. Isn't that a lot?"

4. "Is your boss the main problem around here?"

5. "You planned a 20% cut in costs. Instead they rose 30%. Who's fault is that?"

6. "I hear you cause high turnover in this department. Is that right?"

Appendix **D**

Listening and Reflecting Feeling

Select, or write, the answer which reflects the interviewee's feelings and which moves the interview toward pay dirt.

1. "I've done my best with this department. But what with interference from above and union troublemakers in the ranks I can't seem to meet schedules or keep costs in line."
   a. "You've done your best here."
   b. "Top management's always interfering."
   c. "The union's giving you a hard time."
   d. "You're frustrated in meeting your goals."
   e. Other:

2. "We don't need more computers around here—we're up to our eye balls in data. What we really need are a few decision makers!"
   a. "You've got too many computers here."
   b. "The mass of data is getting in the way."

    c. "You can't see the forest for the trees."
    d. "Nobody makes decisions here."
    e. "Your systems are OK. Your management is not."
    f. "This company is indecisive."
    e. Other:

Respond to the following statements in a way that (a) reflects the interviewee's feeling, and (b) moves the interview toward pay dirt.

3. "I know what my boss has been telling you, but my job is quality control. And I intend to see that we don't produce junk like we used to."

4. "Whenever there's a crunch, it is the training budget they cut first. They don't seem to understand that if we did more training in this company we'd have fewer crunches."

5. "This project you're on is just one more example of top management stupidity—to say nothing of the money we're wasting on you guys. I'm not even sure I want to tell you a damn thing."

Appendix **E**

INTERVIEW PRACTICE USING TRIADS

The following exercise is designed for one or more groups of three, each made up of (1) an interviewer, (2) an interviewee, and (3) an observer. (If the group is not divisible by three, drop or add observers.) Normally a leader (trainer or experienced consultant) runs the exercise and the general discussions and question/answer periods following each interview.

1. Preparation

    Interviewee(s)—Select a position you are thoroughly familiar with, e.g., the position you now hold or the one before it.

        —Tell the interviewer what the company is/was and what your title or role is/was.

    Interviewer(s)—Using the interviewee's company and job, write out your Lead Statement for a 20 min. diagnostic interview to cover responsibilities, assets, problems, and solutions (RAPS). (For a 10–15 min. interview, use RPS only.)

Observer(s)   —Copy the prepared Observer's Check Sheet (see Exhibit 4).

—Observe good things/bad things throughout the interview.

···-Act as timer, including a two minute warning to bring the interview to an end.

2. Conduct Interview, including role play of self-introduction, ice breaking, Lead Statement, topical coverage, and conclusion.

3. Intra-Group Critique

—Observer conducts critique of interviewer

—Interviewee offers reactions and critique ("I felt very comfortable about. . . ," "You might have pushed me more about . . . ," etc.)

—All triads join general discussion about the process.

4. General Discussion

—Leader asks for questions. He may also role play (a) a friend and co-worker of interviewee—"How did it go?" "Did he get at the real problems around here?" "Do you think this outfit can help us improve things here?" "I'm next. What should I watch out for?" And/or (b) the boss or co-consultant of the interviewer—"Did you feel you got at the basic problems?" "What would you handle differently?" "Why not use a questionnaire?" "Would his/her ideas work?"

5. Switch roles and repeat steps 1 through 4.

—Observers become interviewers

—Interviewees become observers

—Interviewers become interviewees

6. Switch again and repeat steps 1 through 4.
(For diads—pairs—the interviewee should act as the observer and provide feedback/critique to the interviewer.)

Using 20 minutes per interview covering four topics (RAPS), this exercise will require at least 1½ hours to run, including 3–4 minutes for preparation of each interview, and 6–7 minutes for post-interview intra-group and general critiques and discussions.

Exhibit 4

OBSERVER'S CHECK SHEET

Comments (plus & minus)

1. Ice Breaker _____
   _____
   _____
   _____
   _____

2. Encouragers, _____
   Pats, etc. _____
   _____
   _____
   _____

3. Probing— _____
   appropriate, _____
   well done _____
   _____

4. Softening of _____
   questions _____
   _____
   _____

5. Spontaneity, _____
   flow _____
   _____
   _____

6. Pay dirt: real _____
   problems and _____
   solutions _____
   _____

BETTER RESPONSES

Appendix A, Drill 2,a—*excessive turnover* causes:
- —poor supervisors
- —no advancement
- —low pay/benefits
- —competitor "raiding"
- —mishiring
- —business decline—real or rumored

Topics to cover causes:

4	Supervisory practices
2	Personnel practices
3	Morale
1	Business prospects

Specific questions:

Topic 1—Current trends regarding sales, profitability
- —Investment in new products or services
- —Company goals
- —Owner succession

87

Topic 2—Competitiveness of pay and benefits
    —Training and development provided by company
    —Promotion policies and practices
    —Hiring practices and standards

Topic 3—Absenteeism and lateness trends
    —Performance standards and controls
    —Attitudes, cooperativeness and communications

Topic 4—Management style
    —Supervisory selection and training practices
    —Opportunity to participate in decisions regarding one's work

Drill 2,b—causes of *excessive audit fees*
    —Poor planning and control of audit
    —Lack of internal controls and/or audits
    —Poor coordination or direction of auditors
    —Poor quality or lack of training of auditors assigned

Topics to cover these causes:

2	Selection and supervision of auditors
4	Internal systems and controls
5	Management letter and auditor findings, comments
1	The audit process—formerly and lately
3	Quality and effectiveness of auditors assigned

Specific questions:

Topic 1—How many auditors assigned, where, for how long
    —Itemize costs and cost trends—what went up
    —Changes in audit process or routines—why

Topic 2—Criteria for selection
    —Who supervises, controls audit teams
    —Company policy regarding changing auditors

Topic 3—Education and experience of auditors assigned
    —Training provided by CPA firm
    —Are audit seniors/supervisors on site

Topic 4—Major systems operating in the company

    —Controls, checks, and balances on these

    —Is responsibility assigned—and system policed

Topic 5—Review comments—current and 2 years back

    —Were these (1) correct, (2) significant/material, and (3) fixed

Drill 2,c—*manufacturing cost overruns*—Lead Statement

"As your department manager's letter stated, our firm has been retained to assist your company in identifying the causes of manufacturing cost overruns, and recommending improvements. In the next hour or so, I'd like to review with you your position here, your organization, the manufacturing processes and controls now being used, and where you believe some improvements can be made."

Lead Questions

Topic 1—"Let's begin with your position—your major responsibilities."

Topic 2—"Next let's review your organization—to whom you report, who reports to you, and how you developed the present structure."

Topic 3—"How about the manufacturing operation—walk me through the various stages and how each is controlled."

Topic 4—"What are some of the major problems here, as you see them?"

Topic 5—"What are some of the ideas or solutions that have occurred to you? Let's begin with . . ."

Appendix B, *Probing*

Question	Answer(s)
1	d, e and f—"You feel poor management is the cause of your low profits."
2	d and e
3	"Let's explore that situation a bit more. (1) You felt you had to put Mary in charge? (2) Who was your

best prospect for the job, and how might this have been handled to minimize the risk of Mary leaving?"

4   "Do you feel the problem is runaway costs or a communication barrier with the DP Manager—or perhaps they are linked?"

5   "Let's talk about company goals and how your R&D role fits in. What was your original understanding about this, and how has it changed?"

6   "The manufacturing function gets flack from sales and engineering?" "Let's begin with your plant and how you manage it—and then go on to some of the possible disagreements with sales and engineering."

Appendix C, *Softening*

Question	Answer
1, a	"What might have accounted for the overrun in this year's capital budget?"
1, b	"Let's talk a little bit about the capital budgeting process here—how it is made up, approval steps, controls, etc."
2, a	"Would you say that there might be times when a little more firmness on your part might have gotten better results?"
2, b	"Let's talk about management style—the ways in which managers direct and monitor the work of their subordinates."
2, c	"As a manager where do you feel your approach is most effective; and where do you feel some training might help you do a little better—your problem areas?"

---

3   "Let's talk about your management approach—how you are able to direct and monitor the work of your people. With 40 subordinates you must have your hands full."

4   "A number of the problems you have mentioned seem to originate with your boss. Is it his style, is he

overworked, does it come down on him from higher up—or just how would you diagnose the main problem here?" (Alternate: "Let's talk about your boss. What are the things he does best, and where might he stand a little improvement?")

5   "What might have accounted for the unplanned rise in costs this year?"

6   "You mentioned that you or the Personnel Department talked to those who left the company this year. What were some of the causes they brought up—and do you agree or disagree with the things they listed?"

Appendix D, *Listening and Reflecting Feeling*

Question	Answer
1	d
2	d

----

3   "You feel your boss wants you to ease up on QC."

4   "Training doesn't get the support it deserves."

5   "You feel management should be solving its own problems." Followed by, "And what might some of these be?"

ABOUT THE AUTHOR

John Quay formed Quay Associates in 1976 after twenty-five years of consulting and in-company experience in personnel and organization work. His in-company experience includes positions as an Executive Recruiter for GE and in personnel management with American Airlines and Curtiss-Wright.

As a consultant, Mr. Quay has worked for a psychological testing and executive search firm, Coopers & Lybrand and Arthur Young & Company. Consulting clients have included GE, The New York Times, The Providence Journal, the Woods Hole Oceanographic Institution, Fidelity Management & Research Corporation in Boston, and a wide variety of manufacturing, retail, government and non-profit institutions.

Mr. Quay grew up in Cairo, Egypt—his father was with the YMCA there—and was educated at Deerfield Academy, Princeton University, and Union Theological Seminary. He has done graduate work in psychology and was trained in personnel assessment by the Psychological Corporation in New York City. He is a Certified Management Consultant and teaches interviewing for the Institute of Management Consultants' "Fundamentals of Management Consulting" Workshops.

ORDER FORM

For orders up to 10 copies, *Diagnostic Interviewing* is priced at $18.75 per copy. The book is available at discount prices for volume purchases as follows:

> 10 to 19 copies @ 10% off = $16.88 each
> 20 to 39 copies @ 20% off = $15.00 each
> 40 or more copies @ 30% off = $13.12 each

To place your order tear out and mail the form below to:

> Quay Associates
> Box 18052
> Columbus, Ohio 43218

Quay Associates
Box 18052
Columbus, Ohio 43218

Quantity   Total

_____ @ $ _____ each = $ _____

       Enclose check with order.

Name _____

(*please print*)

Address _____

City _____ State _____ Zip _____

Ohio residents include 6% sales tax.